NO LONGER
ANYTHINK
RANGEVIEW LIBRARY DISTRICT

THE YOUNG ADULT'S GUIDE TO

Starting a Small Business

101 Ideas for Earning Cash on Your Own Terms

Atlantic Publishing Editorial Staff

THE YOUNG ADULT'S GUIDE TO STARTING A SMALL BUSINESS: 101 IDEAS FOR EARNING CASH ON YOUR OWN TERMS

Copyright © 2017 Atlantic Publishing Group, Inc.

1405 SW 6th Avenue • Ocala, Florida 34471 • Phone 800-814-1132 • Fax 352-622-1875
Website: www.atlantic-pub.com • Email: sales@atlantic-pub.com
SAN Number: 268-1250

No part of this publication may be reproduced, stored in a retrieval system, or transmitted in any form or by any means, electronic, mechanical, photocopying, recording, scanning, or otherwise, except as permitted under Section 107 or 108 of the 1976 United States Copyright Act, without the prior written permission of the Publisher. Requests to the Publisher for permission should be sent to Atlantic Publishing Group, Inc., 1405 SW 6th Avenue, Ocala, Florida 34471.

Names: Atlantic Publishing Group, editor.
Title: The young adult's guide to starting a small business : 101 ideas for earning cash on your own terms / Atlantic Publishing Editorial Staff.
Description: Ocala, Florida : Atlantic Publishing Group, Inc., [2017] | Includes bibliographical references and index.
Identifiers: LCCN 2017028395 (print) | LCCN 2017040119 (ebook) | ISBN 9781620231623 (ebook) | ISBN 9781620231616 (alk. paper) | ISBN 1620231611 (alk. paper)
Subjects: LCSH: New business enterprises. | Small business—Management. | Self-employed.
Classification: LCC HD62.5 (ebook) | LCC HD62.5 .Y665 2017 (print) | DDC 658.1/1—dc23
LC record available at https://lccn.loc.gov/2017028395

LIMIT OF LIABILITY/DISCLAIMER OF WARRANTY: The publisher and the author make no representations or warranties with respect to the accuracy or completeness of the contents of this work and specifically disclaim all warranties, including without limitation warranties of fitness for a particular purpose. No warranty may be created or extended by sales or promotional materials. The advice and strategies contained herein may not be suitable for every situation. This work is sold with the understanding that the publisher is not engaged in rendering legal, accounting, or other professional services. If professional assistance is required, the services of a competent professional should be sought. Neither the publisher nor the author shall be liable for damages arising herefrom. The fact that an organization or Web site is referred to in this work as a citation and/or a potential source of further information does not mean that the author or the publisher endorses the information the organization or Web site may provide or recommendations it may make. Further, readers should be aware that Internet Web sites listed in this work may have changed or disappeared between when this work was written and when it is read.

TRADEMARK DISCLAIMER: All trademarks, trade names, or logos mentioned or used are the property of their respective owners and are used only to directly describe the products being provided. Every effort has been made to properly capitalize, punctuate, identify, and attribute trademarks and trade names to their respective owners, including the use of ® and ™ wherever possible and practical. Atlantic Publishing Group, Inc. is not a partner, affiliate, or licensee with the holders of said trademarks.

Printed in the United States

PROJECT MANAGER AND EDITOR: Danielle Lieneman
ASSISTANT EDITOR: Kylie Widseth
INTERIOR LAYOUT AND JACKET DESIGN: Nicole Sturk

Reduce. Reuse.
RECYCLE.

A decade ago, Atlantic Publishing signed the Green Press Initiative. These guidelines promote environmentally friendly practices, such as using recycled stock and vegetable-based inks, avoiding waste, choosing energy-efficient resources, and promoting a no-pulping policy. We now use 100-percent recycled stock on all our books. The results: in one year, switching to post-consumer recycled stock saved 24 mature trees, 5,000 gallons of water, the equivalent of the total energy used for one home in a year, and the equivalent of the greenhouse gases from one car driven for a year.

Over the years, we have adopted a number of dogs from rescues and shelters. First there was Bear and after he passed, Ginger and Scout. Now, we have Kira, another rescue. They have brought immense joy and love not just into our lives, but into the lives of all who met them.

We want you to know a portion of the profits of this book will be donated in Bear, Ginger and Scout's memory to local animal shelters, parks, conservation organizations, and other individuals and nonprofit organizations in need of assistance.

— Douglas & Sherri Brown,
President & Vice-President of Atlantic Publishing

Table of Contents

Introduction...11

Chapter 1: What You Need to Know Before
Starting Your Own Business..13

    Are You Up for Self-Employment?.. 13

    The Challenge of Starting a Business as a Student........................... 15

    The Pros and Cons of Self-employment.. 16

    Personal Pros and Cons.. 17

    Failure Rates of Small Businesses 17

    10 Reasons You Should Start a Business 18

    Test Your Idea 19

    Organizations You Can Turn to for Help 22

    Checklist for Starting Your Business 23

Chapter 2: Honoring the Classics 25

    1. Babysitter 25

    2. Cleaning Specialist/Maid..27

    3. House Sitter 30

4. Tutor...*32*

5. Restaurant Delivery Service...*37*

6. Pet Sitter/Dog Walker..*39*

7. Animal Trainer..*42*

8. Gift Wrapper..*44*

9. Laundry Service Specialist...*46*

10. Pet Groomer...*48*

11. Car Washer...*50*

Chapter 3: So You Want to Be a Freelancer?...................................**55**

12. Editor..*55*

13. Writer..*58*

14. Makeup Artist...*62*

15. Graphic Designer..*63*

16. Technical Writer..*67*

17. Transcriptionist..*69*

18. Voice-Over Actor..*71*

19. Web and Mobile Designer..*72*

20. Logo Designer...*74*

21. Photographer..*75*

22. Translator...*78*

23. Email and Marketing Automation..*79*

24. Telemarketing and Telesales..*80*

25. SEO—Search Engine Optimization..*81*

26. Customer Service..*83*

27. Ebook Producer/Publisher...*84*

28. Professional Researcher...86

29. Illustrator 87

Chapter 4: Channel Your Creative Side.................89

30. Fashion Designer..89

31. Event Planner...92

32. Floral Designer...94

33. Craft Show Organizer 96

34. Gift Basket / Crate Designer..97

35. Interior Decorator 99

36. Disc Jockey.. 101

37. Scrapbooker 103

38. Picture Framer... 104

39. Costume Designer 106

40. Music Lessons.. 108

41. Painter (Artist) 110

Chapter 5: DIY Junkies Unite!..............................113

42. Upcycling...113

43. Jewelry Designer..115

44. Candle making 117

45. Seamstress/Tailor...119

46. Potter 121

48. Creating a Makeup Line.. 125

49. Crafting Scented Wax Tarts for Burners....................... 128

50. Reupholstering/Refinishing Furniture........................... 130

52. Coffee Mug Designer 134

Chapter 6: If You're a People Person 137

53. *Lounge Owner* *137*

54. *After School Program Worker* *140*

55. *Professional Fundraiser* *142*

56. *Personal Concierge* *143*

57. *Marketing Assistant* *145*

58. *Teach Swimming Lessons* *146*

59. *Activist* *150*

60. *Spa Parties Consultant* *152*

61. *Campaign Manager* *154*

62. *Elder Supervisor* *156*

63. *Consultant* *158*

64. *Manicurist* *159*

65. *Hairstylist* *161*

66. *Trivia Night Host* *163*

67. *Personal Trainer* *165*

Chapter 7: #hashtags and the Internet: Options for the Digitally Savvy 167

68. *Social Media Influencer* *167*

69. *Technology Consultant/Helper* *169*

70. *App Creator* *172*

71. *Virtual Assistant* *174*

72. *Smartphone Repair* *175*

73. *Computer Repair Specialist* *177*

74. *Videographer* *180*

75. *Bookkeeper* *184*

76. Tax Services 185

77. YouTuber 187

78. Blogger 190

79. E-Commerce/eBay Reseller 194

80. Stock Photo Seller 196

81. Device Creator 198

Chapter 8: For the Foodies 201

82. Caterer 201

83. Personal Chef 203

84. Cake Decorator 205

85. Farmer's Market Food Seller 208

86. Cooking Show Creator 209

87. Candy-maker 212

88. Food Truck Owner/Operator 214

Chapter 9: If You Have Muscles 217

89. Moving Services 217

90. Appliance/Furniture Deliverer 219

91. Organizer 221

92. Junk Remover 223

93. Automotive Detailer 225

94. Snow Shoveler 227

95. Lawn Service 228

96. Gardening Service 230

Chapter 10: In Case You *Still* Haven't Found
Your Niche...233

    97. Astrologer...*233*

    98. Talent Agent *235*

    99. Mystery/Secret Shopping Specialist *236*

    100. Consignment Shop Owner *238*

    101. Product Manufacturer *240*

Chapter 11: How to Finance Your Business............................245

    Forms of Financing *246*

    Additional Forms of Financing *247*

    Business Tips, Information, and Resources for Students..................*249*

    Financing – Where to Apply for and Get Your Financing.............*251*

Conclusion..253

Bibliography 255

Index...257

Introduction

While your friends are applying for jobs at the local supermarket, you have a fire in you for something more. The thought of working for someone else makes your eyes twitch, and you're a natural-born leader.

You, my friend, were born to start your own business. You might be thinking something like, "yeah, right, sounds great, but I'm way too young." That's where you're wrong. This book is full of 101 small business ideas with case studies from people just like you that managed to hit the ground running.

Each chapter is a category of business ideas, and each idea has the following features:

- Business Overview: This will tell you the basics — what the job is, introductory information, and the like.

- Education/Skills: This will highlight any licenses or special education/coursework that might be required.

- Realistic Expectations: We'll be honest with you and discuss how tough it is to actually be successful with this business idea.

- Making Bank: This one is hard because there are so many variables, but we'll give you a general idea as to how much you can expect to earn starting out.

- Case Study: Many of the business ideas in this book aren't just pipe dreams—we've interviewed teens and young business owners, and they explain their stories.

- Business Equipment: Sometimes, a business requires you to have some materials and equipment, which might mean you need to make an initial investment.

- Marketing Tips: Where should you put your time and effort to get clients?

- Additional Resources: If a certain idea really strikes you, check out the additional resources. These will lead you to an organization associated with the idea, others who are successful in their business so you can see what they're doing, or articles that further explain the idea and can lead you in the right direction.

Also, keep in mind that this book is supposed to give you some awesome ideas. The entire Atlantic Publishing Editorial Team came together and crafted all of this up for you — but your job doesn't stop here. Every business idea in this book could be a whole book in itself, so if you find a few that you're interested in, be sure to check out the additional resources.

Let's get started!

Chapter 1

What You Need to Know Before Starting Your Own Business

Starting a business is not for a select group of people or privileged individuals. You do not have to come from a family who previously owned a business, nor do you have to have a business degree. Anyone who has devotion and drive, a passion for success, and an understanding of business concepts can run a business.

If you have no idea what type of business you would like to run, we have provided you with detailed information on over 100 businesses that have a history of success. We have found a way to make it easy for students to find that perfect income before earning their degree.

Are You Up for Self-Employment?

Self-employment is not for everyone; you will have to decide if self-employment is the best thing for you. It is important to get feedback from your family and those closest to you. Allow them to address the concerns and thoughts they may have about your venture. Building a business takes a lot of dedication in the first year.

Considering your current role as a student, list what you specifically think you would gain from starting your own business:

_____

_____

_____

_____

_____

_____

While starting your own business offers many advantages, as a student there are some very specific advantages to starting a business, including:

- ☑ **Financial Freedom**: When you work for someone else you get paid only for the time you actually work. When you work for yourself, you make money 24 hours a day, 7 days a week — especially if you are selling on the web.

- ☑ **Flexible Hours**: When you work for yourself you have the advantage of creating a schedule that can bend or change as necessary so you can maintain your current school schedule. You can work more during breaks and take time off for exam week.

- ☑ **Your Time, Your Training**: When you work for yourself, you decide what is important for you to know. You will earn hands on training in a variety of subjects. In a corporate job you would be limited to one job and one set of duties and responsibilities.

☑ **Responsibility**: As your own boss, you are responsible for the successes or disappointments you face. If you are working for someone else, you are giving that person entire control over your situation. By taking control of your future, you have no one to blame but yourself for your difficulties. On the other hand, you have no one to praise but yourself when you create a successful and marketable business.

☑ **Experience:** Owning your own business will give you the experience you need to succeed in any endeavor in the future, even if your business fails.

We have dedicated an entire chapter to self-evaluation so you can gain some insight into your personal and professional characteristics and to help you figure out the right business and the right process to take for starting your business.

The Challenge of Starting a Business as a Student

The one major challenge that young entrepreneurs face is finding enough startup money. Many banks or lenders won't give a loan to a young person. You may have to consider getting a loan from a family member to get your business rolling.

Young entrepreneurs work fewer hours, take more vacations, and tend not to have any employees. They also have the freedom to perform jobs at their own pace and on their own schedule — all characteristics that indicate their business will be successful.

The Pros and Cons of Self-employment

Of course, everything has a good side and bad side. That is life. There was no way we could create this book without looking at the pros and the cons to help you make a well-informed decision.

PROS	CONS
You are your own boss	You will only have yourself to lean on
You will know exactly where your money is going	The first year there will be no steady income
Tax breaks and tax benefits	You have to do all your own accounting
More freedom with your schedule	You have to set your own schedule and keep everything in line
You gain more personal exposure by selling for yourself and not someone else	Start up costs are expensive

Personal Pros and Cons

Now that we have given you an example of some of the pros and cons, it is time for you to give this exercise a try. Write down your own personal pros and cons in regard to starting and running your own business.

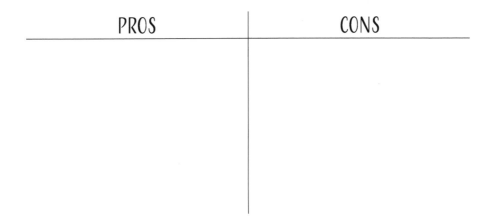

PROS	CONS

Failure Rates of Small Businesses

GardenerBusiness.com states that businesses fail at a 90 percent rate in their first year of operation. This is a staggering figure if you are looking to start your own business. If you look at it from almost any perspective, that number will give you doubts about putting your time and effort into starting a business.

You do not have to be alarmed by that statistic. Instead, be aware that you are starting out fresh and with one of the best tools behind you: *101 Ideas For Earning Cash on Your Own Terms.* There are a number of reasons why companies fail. One of the biggest reasons that small businesses fail is an inadequate or not thought out business plan, which is why we have included a chapter on business plans.

Top reasons why businesses fail:

- Not a defined enough business plan

- Money runs out before the business can start its earnings

- Inadequate business management

- Business owners get discouraged

- Other obligations unforeseen by the owner

Top reasons businesses succeed:

- Owners believe in themselves and their product/service

- Owners don't give up when things start to get tough

- Owners don't take no for an answer.

DID YOU KNOW?

Beloved children's author Dr. Seuss' first book was rejected by the first 27 publishers he sent it to.

The one thing that needs to be emphasized in this chapter is that you should learn everything you can about starting a business, running and maintaining a business, before you think of anything else. To make it successful you need to dot your i's and cross your t's.

10 Reasons You Should Start a Business

We all need a little push now and then to get started toward our goals and dreams. Although we want to be honest about the obstacles you will be facing while starting, running, and maintaining your business, we also want to outline the benefits. We have put together a list of the top ten reasons why you should get started turning your business into reality:

1. Living your dreams

2. Having the flexibility to work, maintain your school schedule, and other things

3. The initial investment is low

4. You decide everything

5. No commute – save on gas

6. You have time for family, other hobbies

7. You are spending your time doing something you love

8. Having the extra money for personal expenses

9. You actually do not have to retire

10. Have something to brag about on your résumé

Test Your Idea

After you have decided to go into business for yourself and before you begin creating the business from scratch, a good plan would be to first test your business concept. There are a few different ways you can do this:

1. Get in touch with family and friends

2. Create a mail marketing questionnaire

3. Contact potential customers

4. Ask strangers

Your family and friends can offer great insight into whether your business idea will work. Knowing them on a personal level will make it easier for you to explain your concept and how you plan to make your business idea happen. They may be able to add some favorable insight into what would make your business better or more marketable.

When you do address your family and friends you want to be in a casual setting. Ask them about the business as you would ask how your outfit looks on you, subtle but serious.

Sometimes it is nice to get some of your most important questions answered like:

1. How well will the public like/need my product or service?

2. What percentage of the community would use/want/need my product or service?

3. Who would most use/buy my product or service?

4. How much would individuals be willing to spend on my product or service?

5. How many times a year will my product or service be in demand?

6. How can I make this a product or service my customers will need many times throughout the year?

7. Which income bracket are my clients in?

8. Where will they most likely buy this product: online, in a store, at the mall, and so on?

With a postcard mailing you might not get all the questions you want answered, but you can get the most important ones answered.

If you are interested in putting together a postcard questionnaire in which potential customers or community members would answer the questions and send it back to you, contact your local office store (Kinkos, Staples, Office Depot, Office Max, and so on), and ask about putting something together. These stores will be able to offer you a variety of options. Whether you send out a flyer or a postcard, be sure to include the postage for the client to send the questionnaires back to you.

You can obtain mailing list information from an organization that provides lists by category, such as Lists Are Us (**www.listsareus.com**) or USA Data (**www.usadata.com**). You can expect one out of every ten to come back to you. Therefore, if you need around 100 responses, you should send out at least 1,000.

A helpful tool for setting up your business involves understanding your potential clients. If they are small business owners, contact some in your area and explain your intention for your business: how you plan to better assist them, how your service/product is different than the competition's, and how you can save them money in that area. Their advice and enthusiasm for your idea can help you better determine and adjust your business plan.

Strangers are biased bystanders. Screenwriters are known to ask people in line at a grocery store or gas station if they would be interested in seeing a movie about their idea. Some may be honest and helpful; others may not want to be bothered, but there is the potential to garner some opinions. Although some people may not be as enthusiastic as you, surveying random people is a helpful option to explore.

Organizations You Can Turn to For Help

You will find a number of organizations available to help you obtain your dream. Whether through the internet or local office branches in your community, there are a number of organizations that will help you start a business, polish or review your business plan, advise you on obtaining financial assistance and support, and give you information on running or expanding your business.

Small Business Resources

A site written by and for entrepreneurs who share their first-hand knowledge of how to succeed in small business. Free, helpful advice from small business and internet experts: **www.smallbusinessresources.com**.

The IRS

Small Business Resources provided by the IRS. Tons of information for the small business owner, as well as up-to-date information about tax incentives and new programs for the small business. This site also offers free software to the small business owner: **www.irs.gov**.

The United States Small Business Administration

The Small Business Administration is another government-run Web portal with business planners, tools, resources, and articles for the small business owner: **www.sba.gov**.

All Business

All Business provides articles with advice for small business owners, as well as a selection of common forms and various resources and links: **www.all-business.com**.

Checklist for Starting Your Business

The following checklist does not only apply to this chapter; you can use this throughout your startup year.

☑ **The Ground Work**

   ☐ Acquire the perfect business for you

   ☐ Access the startup costs

   ☐ Determine your goals (both personal and business)

   ☐ Determine financial resources

   ☐ Establish a marketing plan

   ☐ Identify your potential customers

   ☐ Research your competition

   ☐ Write a business plan

   ☐ Choose your business name

☑ **The Startup**

   ☐ Establish your home office

   ☐ Set up a business account

☐ File for an employee identification number (this is used like your business's social security number; you must have one)

☐ Register your business (the business name with your state)

☐ Incorporate your business

☐ Obtain licensing (if needed)

☐ Obtain insurance (if needed)

☐ Hire professionals in the areas you need help in

☑ **The Opening**

☐ Set an opening date

☐ Plan an opening celebration

☐ Advertise

☐ Get business cards

☐ Acquire all necessary inventory

☐ Join a professional group or organization

☐ Purchase signs

Chapter 2

Honoring the Classics

The classics are classics for a reason. These beloved small business ideas have been successful to many teens for many generations. Since these ideas are the most popular, you'll be able to find a lot of help online (from advice to business plans to helpful resources). These may not be the most unique ideas in the book, but if you're looking for a low risk, high reward business, one of these businesses might be for you.

1. Babysitter

Business Overview

Taking care of kids is one of the most tried-and-true teenage jobs because it's simple and always in demand. There are a ton of reasons why parents may need a babysitter—they might have to pull an all-nighter at the office, there could be a family emergency, or maybe they just want to enjoy a relaxing night out with some friends. Parents need a reliable and responsible individual they can trust to watch their kids; if you're that type of person, babysitting can be a very rewarding business.

Education/Skills

Like all jobs that involve children, babysitters need to be friendly, responsible, creative, and patient. But most of all, they need to be dependable.

Being CPR and first-aid certified isn't mandatory, but it's definitely a plus if you want to rise above the competition. Having these certifications under your belt not only shows that you take your job seriously, but it assures parents that their children are in good hands. A training course only takes a few hours out of your day and usually doesn't cost more than 30 dollars.[1] For the safety and confidence it provides, it's well worth the investment.

Realistic Expectations

For most teenagers, breaking into the babysitting business is quick and painless. If you let a few family friends know that you're available, you can easily land your first few jobs — which can then lead to others. Parents don't need a babysitter every night, so you will need a long client list if you want steady work.

Also, to the guys, keep in mind that this is a female-dominated market.[2] You may find that it's harder to get a job in this area when you first start out.

Making Bank

Depending on the length of the job and how many kids you have to manage, the average babysitter can expect to make anywhere between 10 and 15 dollars an hour.[3]

---

1. Williams, 2015.
2. Dahr, 2014.
3. Smith, 2017.

Business Equipment

There is no business equipment needed.

Marketing Tips

Get the word out! Distribute fliers, put ads in your community newspaper, ask for referrals from friends and family members, announce your services on social media, and take advantage of apps like Sitter and sites like **www .care.com**. If you do a good job, the word will spread.

Additional Resources

www.sittingaround.com

www.sittercity.com

www.urbansitter.com/mobile

2. Cleaning Specialist/Maid

Business Overview

A clean house is a work of art. It takes the right person, the right tools, and a fair amount of time and patience to get the piece done right. Cleaning is tough, but if you have a knack for it, people will pay top dollar for your services.

A cleaning specialist isn't limited to cleaning houses; they also clean apartments, office buildings, restaurants, and other commercial buildings. Most people don't realize that large corporations hire cleaners to deep clean once a week. Whether you work on family houses or commercial buildings, your duties will include things like:

- Sweeping and mopping floors

- Cleaning debris

- Scrubbing baseboards

- Emptying trash

- Dusting and polishing furniture

- Vacuuming carpets

- Deodorizing rooms

- Disinfecting toilet areas

- Cleaning windows

Education/Skills

The only skills you need are a strong work ethic, the ability to clean well, and a dedication to your business.

Realistic Expectations

Most cities have plenty of professional cleaning services to choose from, but this doesn't mean you should be afraid to throw your hat in the ring. You may not have access to high-tech, deep-cleaning equipment, but there are hundreds of clients who only want the basics. With competitive rates, along with a little advertising and networking, you can easily get these people's business.

Making Bank

The average house cleaner can expect to make anywhere between 25 to 45 dollars an hour — and sometimes more.[4]

Business Equipment

You will need to bring your own supplies to each client. Some essentials are vacuum cleaners, brooms, mops, face masks, rubber gloves, knee pads, and commercial strength cleaning products — most of which can be purchased through a janitorial supply store.

---

4. HomeAdvisor, 2015.

Marketing Tips

To get your cleaning service off the ground, you need to target a specific niche. What sort of buildings do you want to clean? What type of cleaning do you want to do? Once you've decided on your niche, make sure the area where you want to work has enough potential customers.

When you first start out, let all your friends, relatives, and neighbors know about your business. This is a quick way to get referrals and start cleaning. But if you want your client base to grow, you will need to develop a professional image and advertise it. Distribute well-made fliers and business cards, put ads in your community newspaper, and set up a website and social media pages so customers can share with others and post reviews.

Additional Resources

www.hloom.com/download-free-house-cleaning-flyer-templates/

www.atyourbusiness.com/forms.php

www.aromatherapynaturals.com/pages/cleaning-resources

3.   House Sitter

Business Overview

When people go on vacation, what happens to their home? Are their personal belongings safe? Are their pets and plants taken care of? A house sitter offers their traveling clients peace of mind while they are away. Some of the most common house-sitting duties include:

- Pet care
- Gardening

- Mowing the lawn

- Deterring robbers

- Retrieving the mail

- Keeping the home neat and tidy

- General maintenance

Education/Skills

There are no educational skills needed for this business opportunity. However, if you have any experience with pets, lawn care, or general maintenance, put these on your résumé so you stand out from the crowd.

Realistic Expectations

Although the house-sitting business is cheap to run and has a high chance of repeat customers, it's difficult to make more than a supplemental income unless you plan to hire employees and grow the business into a house-sitting referral service. Still, there will always be a high demand for house sitters (especially for homeowners with pets), and it remains a good way to make some money.

Making Bank

There are many factors to consider when it comes to house-sitting rates. How long are you house sitting? What are your duties? Are there pets?

Some people house sit in exchange for a place to stay while traveling, while others charge per night, per week, per month, or per project. Depending on these responsibilities, short-term house sitters can expect to make about

$12.29 an hour.[5] Long-term house sitters can easily make $500 or more per project.

Business Equipment

There is no business equipment for this position.

Marketing Tips

Create ads for newspapers, post your services on websites, put fliers in community centers, ask for referrals from friends and family members, announce your new business on social media, and take advantage of house-sitting sites like HouseCarers.com and TrustedHouseSitters.com.

Additional Resources

www.housesittersamerica.com

www.mindmyhouse.com

www.caretaker.org

4.   Tutor

Business Overview

Do you enjoy working one-on-one with others? Are you patient? Do you work well with children? If so, tutoring could be a very rewarding experience. Tutors can make a huge difference in people's lives by working with individuals and helping them through a wide range of subjects. Some common areas where people need tutors include:

---

5. PayScale, 2017.

- Reading

- English

- Math

- Music

- Computers

- Science

- History

- Government

- College Prep

Education/Skills

You need patience to be a tutor. And although a teaching degree is not necessary, any sort of expertise or qualification in your field will increase the odds of obtaining clients. Good communication skills are also a must-have.

Realistic Expectations

There will always be a need for tutors online or in your area. If you have a skill that you know how to teach, potential clients won't be hard to find. Of course, how many clients you get depends on what you're teaching.

Making Bank

Personal instructors usually charge according to their experience and level of education. Tutors make an average of $17.28 an hour.[6]

---

6. Payscale, 2017.

Because of the wide range of subjects and levels of experience, tutors can make anywhere from $20,000 to $80,000 a year.[7]

CASE STUDY:
DANIEL SLONIM

A friend of mine was studying for the SAT. Her mom knew I was good at math, so she asked if I would spend an hour a week tutoring her daughter in math. She offered to pay me $10 an hour, which sounded great to me. I had always loved math, and at the time, I was making $7.25 an hour stocking shelves at a grocery store. I realized this was a way for me to make better money while doing something I really enjoyed. I tutored this friend once a week for most of the summer, and then in September other people started hearing that I was tutoring in math. My mom's cousin asked me to tutor her son, who was in algebra 2, and her daughter, who was taking pre-algebra. Another acquaintance asked me to tutor three of her kids, who were all at different levels. By the end of the fall, I was doing enough tutoring that I decided to quit my part-time job at the grocery store in order to focus on my tutoring.

It was really exciting to be able to do what I loved, and I enjoyed the challenge of finding new ways to try to get clients.

My goal was to save some money for college while leaving myself enough time to do my own schoolwork. When business was at its peak, I was making around $100 a week. It wasn't quite as much as I would have made if I had stayed with my grocery job, but it was pretty close.

I'd usually meet for an hour a week with my students to talk about questions they had about their homework. If they were studying for the SAT, they would take practice tests, go over the questions they got wrong, and then ask me to explain the ones they couldn't understand. I charged $10 to $12 per hour per student.

7. Payscale, 2017.

My most successful advertising was by word of mouth. I walked into a school to ask if I could put up a flier on a bulletin board somewhere, and the receptionist at the school said she had a son who needed tutoring. I don't think I even ended up being able to put up the flier, but I tutored her son for several weeks.

My parents were very supportive, and they gave me lots of encouragement. The most tangible way they helped was by letting me borrow the family van to drive to students' houses, since I didn't have my own car.

Start small, and work your way up from there. I was able to keep a part-time job until my business had grown enough that I knew it was profitable, and that was really helpful. Also, don't feel like you have to be making thousands of dollars to be successful. As long as you're making anything, it's worth it, and the experience of running your own business is valuable.

Daniel Slonim is currently a doctoral student in mathematics at Purdue University. He still does some tutoring on the side.

Business Equipment

Equipment will vary depending on your subject. You may need a computer, reference books, musical instruments, study guides, laptops, software, notebooks, paper, pencils, pens, etc.

Marketing Tips

How you market your tutoring business depends a lot on the sort of tutoring you offer. What are you teaching? Who do you want to teach? Do you want to travel to clients' houses or do you want clients to come to you? Do you want to teach solely over the internet? Once you've answered these kinds of questions, you'll have a better idea of how to market your services.

Post fliers in community centers, libraries, bulletin boards in your school, and other places where families and students will see them. You can even ask schools to refer students to you. Create your own blog or website, put ads in your local newspaper, advertise on websites like Craigslist and Upwork.com, ask for referrals from friends and family members, announce your tutoring service on social media, and take advantage of tutoring sites like **TakeLessons.com** and **Care.com**.

Additional Resources

www.mytopbusinessideas.com/starting-a-tutoring-business

www.wyzant.com

https://buddyschool.com

5. Restaurant Delivery Service

Business Overview

Many high-class restaurants do not offer delivery services, but if you have a reliable vehicle, you can offer delivery service. They make the order, and you pick it up and deliver it.

If you've got a car and a good driving record, you could build a business delivering delicious food to people in their homes in your local area.

Education/Skills

Other than a driver's license, there's not a lot of skill or education required to do this job. You may need to brush up on your negotiating skills since you will have to work out how you're getting paid. If you're particularly tech-savvy, you could design your own app to make ordering and payment easier for your customers and possibly make more efficient use of your time.

Realistic Expectations

You'll need to build relationships with restaurants that don't already have delivery service. Focus on local, one-of-a-kind places, and don't bother with franchises or chain restaurants. If you're successful, you may be putting a lot of wear and tear on your personal vehicle, so keep track of your mileage and your vehicle service records for tax purposes. Be sure that what you charge for your service will cover the cost of your overhead. Some kind of app would be your best bet for making the most of your time and would also simplify payment.

Making Bank

Delivery drivers make an average of $13.40 per hour.[8]

Business Equipment

You'll need a reliable vehicle and insulated bags for transporting food. A cash box or money belt of some kind would also be useful, and a smart-phone with a card-reading device is critical.

Marketing Tips

Get your company logo and contact info printed on a t-shirt or jacket, and get some car magnets to brand your vehicle. Everywhere your car goes is an opportunity to advertise. Leave flyers at the restaurants you partner with, at local businesses, college campuses, and hotels. Don't forget to build a website (with a functional mobile version!) so your customers can find you and order when they're on the go.

Additional Resources

www.smallbusiness.chron.com/start-restaurant-delivery-service -business-4457.html

www.payscale.com/research/US/Job=Pizza_Delivery_Driver/Hourly _Rate

www.cnbc.com/2016/02/19/a-start-up-taking-a-bite-out-of-the-food -delivery-business.html

8. PayScale, 2017.

6.   Pet Sitter/Dog Walker

Business Overview

When you go to parties, do you eventually end up in the corner talking to the cat? Do you avoid eye contact with humans, but greet dogs with open arms? If either scenario is true, then you could put your love of animals to good use by starting your own pet sitting and/or dog walking business.

Education/Skills

There aren't any legal requirements for this sort of business, but you may be required to obtain a business license in your state. Check with your local Chamber of Commerce or Business Bureau. There are certification programs available for pet care, as well as associations you could join. A certificate or membership in an association may not make a huge difference in your skills, but potential clients will have some proof of your work ethic and determination.

Realistic Expectations

More and more, people are putting their animals' needs first, and you could reap the benefits. Dog walking and pet sitting can be physically strenuous, particularly with younger animals that have a lot of energy to burn. You will probably have to be up quite early and sometimes very late, and you should take notes about any animal's needs (dietary restrictions, medications, etc). You may also want to look into business insurance to cover yourself in case you are injured by an animal, as well as liability insurance in case an animal is injured while in your care. You may be an animal-lover and a very careful person, but accidents don't discriminate, so make sure you're taking every step you can to be safe for yourself and for your clients.

Making Bank

The average salary of a pet sitter is $12.69 an hour.[9]

I don't remember exactly when watching our neighbors' dogs became an annual summer ritual for my sister and me, but I think the neighbor suggested it to my mom one day when my sister and I were in middle school. I remember my mom coming back on a warm summer evening from a chat with the neighbor, and she said, "Rachel and Rebekah, would you like to watch Dave and Sue's dogs while they go on vacation?"

Rachel and I—like many enterprising youngsters—had considered dog sitting before, and, while the job wasn't our own idea, we were delighted about the opportunity.

I liked the flexibility, the independence, and the chance to practice some problem-solving. We earned several hundred dollars each summer.

We went over to Dave and Sue's house three times a day—once in the morning, before the sun was completely up, to let the dogs out and feed them breakfast; once in the afternoon, for a long chunk of time, to pet them and give them attention as we read books and chatted; and once in the evening to feed them supper, let them out again, and encourage them to lie down and go to sleep.

It was always satisfying to get a nice wad of cash when Dave and Sue came back. My family always placed a big emphasis on budgeting well and saving money, so I enjoyed the chance to manage a small income of my own that I could divide into saving, giving, and spending portions. I also enjoyed

9. PayScale, 2017.

all the dog cuddles and earning the trust of the dogs. It was really reward-ing to see them respond to our care and attention.

Try to get a regular dog sitting job and stick with it. My family has a dog, too, and we know how nice it is to have a dog sitter who is reliable and depend-able. If you have a habit of saying yes whenever you're asked to dog sit, it's a great way to get steady work.

Rebekah Slonim and her sister Rachel did dog sitting for their neighbors for nearly a decade until they moved away from their hometown of Columbus, Ohio.

Business Equipment

Depending on your location, you will probably need a vehicle, or some kind of reliable transportation. Also, any self-respecting pet owner should have their own collars, leashes, treats, and waste disposal bags, but it cer-tainly wouldn't hurt you to keep some of your own. Get yourself a sched-uling book or software for keeping track of appointments, and a filing system (digital or analog) for your clients' contact information and any special notes about their animal(s). If you have clients who schedule visits with you each and every day or week, you'll need to keep copies of their house keys and alarm codes.

Marketing Tips

Distribute brochures and business cards door to door, at pet stores, at vet-erinarian offices, and at pet grooming establishments. Find dog trainers, breeders, and kennels in your area to network with. For clients, you might offer a referral bonus, such as one free visit for recommending a friend. Look up similar businesses in your area to get an idea of where you should be with your pricing, but also to see what services they offer that you might also charge for.

Additional Resources

www.petmd.com/dog/training/evr_dg_pet_sitter_dog_walker

www.care.com/c/stories/6030/pet-care-certifications-101/

www.homebusinessforms.blogspot.com/

www.portlandmuttstrut.com/ratespolicies/

www.entrepreneur.com/article/172396

7.   Animal Trainer

Business Overview

You've seen animals on TV who do sophisticated tricks, right? Behind every Lassie, Flipper, and Mr. Ed, there's an animal trainer. You probably won't find many clients who need someone to train their dolphin, but there are plenty of people out there who will pay you to train their pets.

Teaching a dog to sit on command or teaching a kitten to use a litter box may sound easy, but some people don't have the time, patience, or knowledge to get the job done right. If you have experience training and working with animals, then it's time to use that knowledge to make a little money.

Education/Skills

An animal training certification might make you more marketable and ensure a bigger paycheck, but it's not mandatory. To be a great animal trainer, all you need is experience with training animals.

Realistic Expectations

If you live in an area with a lot of companion pets like dogs and cats, animal training jobs should be abundant. You can host training classes at your house, you can travel to your clients' houses, or you can even host classes at community centers. Along with a private practice, it's also possible to find work at animal shelters, farms, zoos, aquariums, animal medical clinics, and pet stores.

Making Bank

Animal trainers usually charge according to their level of experience and education as well as the type of animal they are training and the type of training the owner wants. The average salary of an animal trainer is $11.48 an hour.[10]

---

10. PayScale, 2017.

Business Equipment

Equipment will vary depending on the type of training. You may need to purchase your own training aids, leashes and treats.

Marketing Tips

Post fliers in community centers, dog parks, animal medical clinics, pet stores, and other places where pet owners will see them. You can even ask veterinarians, dog walkers, and shelters to refer clients to you. Create your own blog or website, take out classified newspaper ads, ask for referrals from friends and family members, and announce your animal training service on social media.

Additional Resources

www.apdt.com/

www.dogtec.org/index.php

www.petpartners.org/

www.nadoi.org/howdoi.htm

8.   Gift Wrapper

Business Overview

If you're creative and love making people smile, this business idea might make the cut. There's an art to gift wrapping — it's not just about knowing how to expertly fold the wrapping paper. Attention to detail, having an eye for patterns and colors, and creating embellishments are all part of the fun.

Don't forget about special occasions — you might be able to turn your love for gift wrapping into an event planning gig of sorts. Offer your services for baby showers, weddings, and holiday parties, and you'll be rolling in the dough in no time.

Education/Skills

You don't need any special education to start this business. Valuable skills include the following:

- Ability to network

- Social media knowledge

- Creativity

- Organization

- Patience

Realistic Expectations

This job is very achievable! Utilize social media to your advantage — Pinterest and Instagram are great tools to showcase your designs and creations. The biggest downside to this job is that it can be very seasonal. Expect heavy business for holidays and slow spots in between.

Making Bank

The average salary of a gift wrapper is $9 an hour.[11]

---

11. Glassdoor, 2017.

Business Equipment

You will need to buy enough supplies to have a wrapping station. You'll need different patterns and gift wrap options to suit the tastes of your different clients. You'll also need supplies such as paper cutters, tape, and ribbon wheels.

Marketing Tips

You will need to use social media sites such as Instagram and Pinterest to circulate your creations. Networking will also be key — word-of-mouth marketing will turn your business from an idea to a thriving money-maker. Have business cards and a brochure displaying your creations made to help your networking process.

When you've started to make a name for yourself, start approaching local shops and boutiques, and see if you can get a gig wrapping gifts for their customers.

Additional Resources

www.wrapgurldc.com

www.janemeans.com

www.paperchase.co.uk

9.   Laundry Service Specialist

Business Overview

Also called a linen service specialist, this job is perfect for those who don't mind doing laundry. Your duties include picking up laundry from clients (which can be regular people or businesses) and returning them nice and clean.

Education/Skills

No certifications or coursework needed. Having good customer service skills always helps, and you need to be dependable, especially for repeat clients that will rely on your services.

Realistic Expectations

The only challenge you're sure to face in getting this business off the ground is finding clients who are willing to shell out cash for this service. Most people do their own laundry at home, so your sweet spot will be finding clients that don't have washing appliances at home as well as wealthier and busier clients who simply don't have the time to do their own laundry.

Making Bank

The average salary of a laundry service specialist is $9.27 an hour.[12]

Business Equipment

You need to establish a relationship with a dry cleaning facility in order to make this happen. You would then need a suitable vehicle to hold the laundry. Finally, you'll want bags and plastic hooks to carry the laundry with.

---

12. PayScale, 2017.

Marketing Tips

Establishing a working relationship with an existing dry cleaner or laundromat is key. Have them do the work, and offer up your delivery services. Work with the company to spread the word out. Draft email campaigns for their current clients, and make sure to utilize Facebook and other social media sites.

Additional Resources

Check out how these companies present their services. Modeling your business off of businesses that work is always a great tactic:

www.laundrycareexpress.com/services/services

www.ryanh.fatcow.com/joomla/wedoit4u/v1

www.sarnidrycleaners.com/pickup-and-delivery

10.   Pet Groomer

Business Overview

You've gotta love animals. There's no way around it with this one. If your love surpasses your discomfort or disgust at the down-and-dirty aspects of this job, then you'd be a good fit for the pet grooming profession. You will spend anywhere from thirty minutes to three hours with each and every animal, bathing, brushing, clipping nails, and giving them snazzy haircuts.

Education/Skills

To be a responsible groomer, you should study dog (and possibly cat) anatomy. Try to find a groomer in your area who has a solid business and who would be willing to train you. Their knowledge and skills will be an invaluable resource for you. Take notes and be willing to help out in any way you can to repay them for their time and effort.

Realistic Expectations

Pet grooming can be a dirty business. Comfortable clothing that doesn't restrict your movement will be important. You will get wet (from water and soap, but also other unmentionable fluids) and absolutely covered in hair. Elderly dogs may need help getting on and off your grooming table, or in and out of the tub, so some bending and lifting will be required. As you probably already know, animal personalities are as varied as human ones. Will you need to rent space or will you do mobile grooming? What do you need for insurance and how much will your equipment cost? Factor all of these things into your pricing to make sure you cover your overhead.

Making Bank

How much you take home depends on how many animals you can groom in one day. If you're a mobile groomer, some of your time will be taken up with travel and setting up or breaking down your work area. You'll see fewer animals, but you can charge more for the convenience of your service. The average salary of a pet groomer is $11.81 an hour.[13]

Business Equipment

For the actual act of grooming you will need: an adjustable-height table, professional ergonomic cutting shears, nail scissors or clippers, and many different types of brushes and combs. You'll need a tub, some kennels, an

---

13. PayScale, 2017.

industrial hairdryer or two, a wet/dry vacuum, pet shampoo . . . and it couldn't hurt to have some treats around, right? A scheduling book or software would be useful for keeping track of appointments, and a filing system for your clients' contact information and any special notes about their pet.

Marketing Tips

Distribute marketing materials door to door, at pet stores, at veterinarian offices, and with dog walkers and pet sitters. Find dog trainers, breeders, and kennels in your area to network with. Try to establish mutually beneficial relationships with them. For clients, you might offer a referral bonus, such as free nail clipping for recommending a friend or a loyalty system that gets them a free or discounted service after x number of full-price services.

Additional Resources

www.doggroomeradvice.com/

www.groomerschoice.com/Grooming-Tools/departments/11/

www.work.chron.com/average-salary-professional-dog-groomers -3219.html

11.   Car Washer

Business Overview

Cars offer all sorts of business opportunities, and car washing is one of the fastest and easiest gigs to get off the ground.

As a car washer, you will do just that — wash cars. You can do this at a fixed location and let the cars come to you, or you can start a mobile car washing business and travel to your customers.

Education/Skills

You don't need any special education to start this business. If you can make a car shine, you're golden.

Realistic Expectations

Getting into the car washing industry is almost too easy. Every day cars drive down dirt roads, splash through mud puddles, or get special presents from birds. If you are a hard worker, a good advertiser, and live in a well-populated area, you will find cars to wash. Startup costs are low, there isn't a lot of competition on the hand-washing level, and most people are more than happy to pay someone to do their dirty work for them.

Making Bank

What you charge to wash a vehicle depends on a lot of different factors. What kind of cleaning do you do? How long will it take? How dirty is the vehicle? Is it a small car or a massive SUV? How much are your cleaning products? And, most importantly, what do you think your labor is worth? The average salary of a car washer is $10.87 an hour.[14]

Business Equipment

There's a lot that goes into cleaning a car. Some basic tools you will need include a water source, sponges, brushes, car wash soap, all-purpose cleaner,

---

14. Chron, 2017,

buckets, micro-fiber cloths, shammys, towels, tire dressing, wheel and tire cleaner, squeegees, bug and tar remover, degreaser, extension cords, a vacuum cleaner, a receipt book, and a vehicle if you are driving to your customers.

Marketing Tips

A good way to get the ball rolling on any business is to offer your services for free or at a discount. Visit restaurants, beauty salons, barber shops, and neighborhoods to hand out fliers that describe your business as well as your special promotions. Be prepared to wash cars on the spot. This will allow you to introduce yourself to potential customers, get the word out, and show off your car-washing skills.

You can also stand on the side of the road with a sign directing cars to your car wash or put up posters in community centers, libraries, laundromats, and other places where people will see them. To get even more attention, create a blog or website, take out classified newspaper ads, ask for referrals from friends and family members, and announce your service on social media.

Additional Resources

www.carwash.com/

www.washos.com/blog/mobile-car-wash-business/

www.autowash.com.au/car-wash-building-construction/

Chapter 3

So You Want to Be a Freelancer?

The beauty about freelancing is that most of the time, you can do it from home. If you're shy or are particularly word- or design-savvy, you might find your perfect small business idea here. While "freelancing" might immediately cause you to think of editing, writing, or design, you'll come to see that there are many more freelance opportunities out there that cover many skill sets, such as makeup artistry, web design, photography, and even being the voice talent for commercials and audiobooks. The options are wide, so let's take a look at the possibilities.

12. Editor

Business Overview

If you have a knack for grammar and punctuation, being a freelance editor is a great way to build up your skills and resume while also making money. There are a lot of sites out there that have job listings, the most recommended one being Upwork.com. You need to create a profile and outline your most relevant skills.

Education/Skills

Having a degree in English is ideal, but it's not necessary. It's nice to have a certification such as the one from Writer's Digest (**www.writersonline-workshops.com/courses/copyediting-certification-course**), but if you offer to do a 2-page editing sample for your client, you can prove your worth.

Realistic Expectations

Obtaining a gig doing freelance editing is very realistic. If you want to get some experience under your belt, offer up pro bono editing services to a local nonprofit or church. Chances are they have fliers, manuals, or *some* kind of writing that could use a good editor. One you have that experience, you can start applying to available jobs. We highly recommend the site **www.upwork.com** for finding the perfect fit.

Making Bank

You can make really good money editing, but like anything, you won't be able to charge as much until you have more education and experience under your belt.

The range is very wide, from ambitious authors looking for a cheap set of eyes, to companies looking for a very professional and thorough editor.

The pay for editing work is really hard to standardize, because there are many factors that come into play:

- The budget of the client

- The amount of editing work needed (does it just need a quick grammar check or does it need to be completely restructured?)

- The timeline (is it a rush job or do we have some time?)

- The possibility of recurring work (when this project is done, will the client supply me with more projects?)

The average salary of an editor is $29.08 an hour, but this can vary greatly depending on experience.[15]

Business Equipment

You will need a computer (preferably dual monitor) and a word processing program.

---

15. Chron, 2017.

Marketing Tips

Create an eye-catching resume and fill out your Upwork profile as completely as you can. Also consider optimizing your LinkedIn profile so that when a client searches your name, they are impressed by how professional you are.

Additional Resources

www.copydesk.org

www.spj.org/index.asp

www.upwork.com

13.   Writer

Business Overview

Do you enjoy writing? If you enjoy writing informational articles, interview pieces, feature articles, or newsworthy content, freelance writing can be a fulfilling career for you.

A freelance writer's process is like this:

- They think of the idea or piece to write.

- They research the idea and find focused information on the subject.

- They write the article.

- Research the market to send it to.

- Write a query letter.

- Submit the query letter to a list of potential editors.

- Wait for a reply.

- *If* the editor replies with interest then the writer submits the article.

And this process continues. Freelance writing is a very competitive market, and it can take years before a writer receives his first purchase. Many well-known authors and writers, Stephen King for example, were rejected a number of times before they had their first piece published.

Education/Skills

Excellent good grammar skills are imperative; therefore, an English or creative writing degree would be helpful.

Making Bank

The average salary of a writer is $24.70 an hour.[16]

16. PayScale, 2017.

CASE STUDY:
JESSICA E. PIPER

I started getting paid to write when I was 18. I've always loved writing. In college, I started writing for a student newspaper and a magazine, as well as several blogs. I thought it would be great if I could have the chance to make money doing something I liked, so I started scanning job boards looking for freelance writing opportunities.

Working as a freelance writer allows me to do my work on my own time. While I have to keep to my deadlines, I do my job when it's convenient for me — for example, when I am traveling or on days where I don't have too much other work, as I am still a college student. Before I began writing, I worked at a café, with the same long shifts every Saturday and Sunday, which didn't give me much free time as a full-time student. I like having the freedom to fit my work to my schedule.

My first book got published when I was 19. I remember receiving six copies from my publisher and being amazed to see my own name on the front cover. I also like to tell people to search my name on Amazon because my book comes up. It's pretty cool!

My mom will sometimes read my drafts before I send them to an editor, but that's mostly for fun — more often, she's the one asking me for help when she needs to write something for her job.

My biggest piece of advice is don't underestimate yourself. It's easy to think, "I'm not qualified to do this," but you probably are. In the real world, people often judge you on your abilities — not your age or your level of education. If you think you have a skill or talent that other people would appreciate, go for it. The other major piece of advice I have is to make sure you are OK with the level of compensation you are receiving for your service. Especially when you are young, people may try to pay you very little or take advantage of you in other ways. For example, in the writing world, many places ask you to write but won't pay you — they say you benefit from the "exposure." If you are starting your own business, you probably want to get paid. Make sure you are working with people who recognize this goal and value your time and energy.

Jessica E. Piper is an American writer. She grew up in Colorado before moving to Maine for college. Some of her favorite writing topics include obscure historical happenings, contemporary social issues, and analysis of popular culture. She currently studies economics and works for a weekly college newspaper. When she is not writing, she enjoys music, travel, and spending time with friends and family. You can find her on Twitter @jsscppr.

Business Equipment

Nothing more than basic office equipment is needed.

Marketing Tips

A marketing tool would be to find a small local market. Your church or school's monthly newsletter would be a great starting point; ask the editors if you can write a short informative essay.

Once you are published for the first time, keep that clip on file and continue to query your local newspaper or presses in your area; the more times you get your name in print the better. As you get published, keep all your published clips on file, and when you contact the magazines you would like to get into, send them your published clips. Published clips refer to a copy of the place in the periodical where your name appears, not the entire article. Most editors in major markets want to be sure they are working with an experienced writer.

14. Makeup Artist

Business Overview

Makeup artists are people who do makeup for a variety of occasions; oftentimes they do makeup for special occasions like fashion shows or weddings.

Education/Skills

You don't necessarily have to have any education to be a makeup artist. Some people just have a natural talent for it. But you can also go to cosmetology school if you want to learn more about the techniques of makeup. Another great place to get skills is by watching beauty videos on YouTube! But above all, you have to have a knack for makeup.

Realistic Expectations

As long as you have people to do makeup for, and you know of people who need your expertise, this business can be very successful. Talk to friends and friends of friends to see who is looking to get some help in the makeup department.

Making Bank

The average salary of a makeup artist is $17.25 an hour.[17]

---

17. PayScale, 2017.

Business Equipment

To have a successful business as a makeup artist, you need lots and lots of makeup. You also need to have a variety of different types of makeup along with a variety of different brushes and applicators to use on your clients.

Marketing Tips

It might be helpful to start out by talking to friends and family to see if they or anyone they know has an occasion coming up where they might need a makeup artist. Also, be sure to make business cards. People in public might compliment you on your everyday makeup style; this would be a great opportunity to hand out business cards.

Additional Resources

www.careerinmakeup.com/buildingawebsite

www.qcmakeupacademy.com/2014/09/getting-started-freelance -makeup-artist/

15. Graphic Designer

Business Overview

Graphic designers can do a myriad of freelance work including, but not limited to, the following:

- Book cover design

- Typesetting (or laying out) books

- Designing brochures and other marketing materials

- Designing websites

- T-shirt design

- Leaflets

- Product design

The options are endless—someone designs everything that is designed!

Education/Skills

An art or design degree always helps, but don't worry — what really sells is an amazing portfolio. You also need to be proficient in Adobe software such as Photoshop, Illustrator, and InDesign. These are the programs most clients will want to use.

Realistic Expectations

Doing graphic design work is very realistic. As long as you put effort into creating a portfolio to showcase your skills, you can easily start getting clients. **Upwork.com** is a very valuable tool to see what kinds of projects are out there.

Making Bank

The average salary of a graphic designer is $22.90 an hour.[18]

---

18. Bureau of Labor Statistics, 2016.

CASE STUDY: NICOLE STURK

I started doing freelance graphic design in late 2016.

I have always been creative. I started drawing pictures at a young age. I studied art in school and received a Bachelor's degree in the field. I also love to craft and bake, and I have been blogging for a number of years as well (**www.nikijincrafts.com**). I fell into the field of book publishing when I got a typesetting job after college, which introduced me to typography and book design. Ever since graduating college, it has been a professional goal of mine to work for myself as an independent freelancer. Having a baby and moving across the country gave me the push I needed to finally make it happen. I always imagined I'd work strictly as an illustrator, but all of my past experiences have become a part of my work. Yes, I do some illustration, but I also do typesetting and graphic design, and I continue with the craft blog and other personal projects.

I'm still at the beginning stages, but in just a few months, I am at the point where I am making close to what I did at my office job.

I started out on the website Upwork.com, which is geared toward freelancers. I created a profile and applied to jobs that I found interesting that suited my skills. At first, I had to continually pursue work by cold-emailing potential clients and applying to jobs on Upwork, and I was hired to a few odd jobs here and there. Eventually, I found a few clients that now give me work on a regular basis. I spend my days emailing clients and working on various projects. Some days, I'm designing and laying out a book, and other days I'm sitting at my kitchen table and painting. I do everything from home with just my computer, a printer/scanner, a reliable internet connection, some professional software, and a few art supplies!

I've had to make budget sacrifices to save money. Sometimes, I had to say yes to work that I don't really find all that interesting, but I needed to start making some money. It's getting better now, though. Sometimes I've had to sacrifice my personal time in order to work on projects.

At one point, I realized that things were finally all coming together. I was getting the types of jobs I wanted that allowed me to be creative and independent; I was able to spend more time at home with my daughter; and I was finally able to make an OK living doing what I love.

My parents always supported me since I was young. They let me pursue art in school despite any reservations they may have had about job potential. They always encouraged me in anything I wanted to do, and they were there to help me in any way they could. Now, I have the support of my husband as well, who was the one who really pushed me to start freelancing.

It's really important to develop self-discipline when it comes to time management and work ethic. Focus — one of the hardest things to do when working independently is to keep on track and not get discouraged or distracted. It took me years to finally start freelancing, even though I had wanted to for a while, but when I finally made the leap, it didn't take me as long as I thought it would to get going. Find what it is you are passionate about, but also remain flexible when plans don't go quite as planned.

 *Nicole Sturk was born in South Korea and was adopted along with her two sisters (they're triplets!) by American parents when they were young babies. They grew up all over the country, moving around to such states as Pennsylvania, Utah, Michigan, Alabama, and New Hampshire. She received a Bachelor's degree in Art from BYU-Idaho in 2005. From there, she settled back in New Hampshire and worked in book publishing as a typesetter for a little over 10 years. In 2016, she left her office job and moved with her family to Utah. She decided to pursue freelancing as a means to stay home with her young daughter. Visit her website at **www.nicolejonessturk.com**.*

Business Equipment

You will need design software, the most common one requested by clients being the Adobe Creative Cloud software, which is a monthly subscription giving you access to various programs.

Marketing Tips

It is advised that you create a website or blog showcasing your work. Having a complete Upwork profile as well as a robust LinkedIn account will help you network and get repeat clients.

Additional Resources

Create a profile and start getting freelance work:

www.upwork.com

www.99designs.com

www.toptal.com/designers/graphic

Here are a few examples of great graphic design portfolios:

www.design7studio.com/portfolio

www.youandigraphics.com

www.madebyeno.com/work/freshdirect/

16.　Technical Writer

Business Overview

Technical writing can be a lucrative business because of the amount of information needed for this field, the constant change and upgrade in technology, and the topic being difficult to explain. If you can write about it, you will have a steady income for years to come.

Write and edit a variety of publications concerning the technical fields, including:

- Technical books

- Technical articles for trade magazines

- Publicity materials

- Instruction booklets for hardware and software

- Web site content, including SEO articles and ISO documents

- Policy and procedure manuals

- Brochures, fliers, and other desktop publishing materials

- Marketing pieces

Education/Skills

Knowledge or a background in computers, computer science, medicine, communication, and scientific fields such as chemistry, engineering, and electronics are a necessity for this industry.

Making Bank

The average salary of a technical writer is $33.58 an hour.[19]

Business Equipment

The basic home office equipment, plus reference books and database software, will be needed.

---

19. Bureau of Labor Statistics, 2016.

Marketing Tips

Create business cards to hand out to people. Create a website for yourself that people can request your service on. Also, look for sites online that have freelance job listings for technical writing.

17. Transcriptionist

Business Overview

If you're a fast typer, a good listener, a stickler for proper grammar, and love the idea of working in your pajamas, then get your fingers ready — this could be the perfect business for you.

Transcription involves the simple task of typing what is dictated in a voice recording. Along with medical and legal transcription, other jobs include working with podcasters, lecturers, pastors, interviewers, internet marketers, business owners, and anyone who has audio material that would be valuable in a text format (think essays, books, and website material).

Education/Skills

The best transcriptionists are experienced writers, fast typers, and diligent researchers who are familiar with the work they are transcribing. It's possible to become a transcriptionist without any formal training, but remember: many companies only hire certified or degree-holding transcriptionists when it comes to working with medical and legal material.

Realistic Expectations

This isn't the easiest industry to break into. Medical and legal transcriptionists often need a bit of experience and education under their belt to make a steady income, and general clients are sometimes hard to find. Still, with hard work, advertising, and plenty of referrals and return customers, you may find yourself a profitable little niche.

Making Bank

The average salary of a transcriptionist is $14.04 an hour.[20]

Business Equipment

When creating your transcription space, you will need a computer, an internet connection, word processing software, audio playback software, transcription workflow software, headphones, reference books, style guides, and a USB foot pedal that will allow you to control the recording while keeping your hands free to type.

Marketing Tips

If you don't have any experience as a transcriptionist, reach out to local universities, churches, news stations, doctors, podcasters, law firms, and anyone you can think of that has audio material they might want transcribed. Once you've gained some experience in the field, create a résumé and cover letter detailing your skills and services, and start promoting your business and applying for jobs at transcription companies.

While clients may be elusive, that doesn't mean they're not out there. Make yourself easy to find by making social media posts about your services and creating a blog or website advertising your business and rates.

---

20. PayScale, 2017.

Additional Resources

www.transcriptiongear.com

www.blog.gmrtranscription.com

www.podcastinghacks.com/tips-for-starting-a-transcription-serivce

18. Voice-Over Actor

Business Overview

Do you enjoy acting? Want a way to get into acting without all the red tape and years of waiting to catch a break? Do you have a clear, crisp voice that is unique by nature?

Provide voice recordings from material provided by your clients.

Education/Skills

Good communication and oral skills are a must.

Making Bank

The average salary of a voice actor is $50 an hour.[21]

Business Equipment

Audio recording equipment, headphones, music, microphone, and a digital and analog mixer will be needed, along with the basic home-office equipment

---

21. PayScale, 2017.

Marketing Tips

Find auditions with any of the following audition sites and check for updates of new jobs in the industry.

Additional Resources

www.auditionfinder.com

www.entertainmentcareers.net

www.backstage.com

www.castingaudition.com

www.castingyou.com

www.exploretalent.com

www.productionhub.com

www.stagesource.com

19.   Web and Mobile Designer

Business Overview

Have you ever gone to a website on your smart phone that did not have a mobile version? It can be difficult to see the text or navigate the website. Many companies and businesses are in need of mobile versions for their websites or updated mobile versions. That's where you come in. You will make pitches to companies, businesses, and individuals, offering to design mobile versions of their websites.

Education/Skills

You don't need any degree to apply for freelance mobile design jobs on Upwork — although having a degree in graphic design wouldn't hurt, of course! You'll have to show that you have some documented, useful experience in the area of web graphic design. Try to gain as much experience as you can before you start looking for freelance graphic design jobs.

Realistic Expectations

The field is vast — there are countless websites, some of which don't have mobile versions yet and others than need to be redesigned — but obviously there are a lot of people who have a lot more experience than you do. Just be persistent.

Making Bank

The average salary of a web designer is $50 an hour.[22]

Business Equipment

You will need software like Photoshop. And, of course, you'll need a computer on which to do the work.

Marketing Tips

While the temptation might be to only look for jobs online, think about businesses in your area or people you may know personally who might want someone to design websites for them.

---

22. Chron, 2017.

20.   Logo Designer

Business Overview

You'll be working the freelance channels — from Upwork to Indeed — and using word-of-mouth advertising to try to find jobs that will let you be part of shaping customer reactions.

Education/Skills

The simple fact is that companies prefer that their entry-level logo designers have a degree in graphic design. Maybe you can start taking college classes in graphic design at a nearby community college and get an internship. Be creative and find ways to cultivate your skills. It shouldn't be too hard to be creative — you are an up-and-coming logo designer, after all!

Realistic Expectations

This business would be a great way for you to make some money and to give you experience in the field that you want to enter permanently.

Making Bank

The average salary of a logo designer is $22.90 an hour.[23]

Business Equipment

You may have to pay some money for subscriptions for good photo-editing software and other graphic design must-haves. The good news is that you

---

23. Bureau of Labor Statistics, 2016.

won't have transportation costs or any other costs, really. Once you have the right computer and the right software, you can do everything at home.

Marketing Tips

Persistence, persistence, persistence. The jobs are out there, advertised all over the internet. There are many people with more experience who want those jobs, too. So just keep trying until you get a foot in the door. Don't give up!

21. Photographer

Business Overview

Do you have a passion for taking pictures? Do you know how to angle your camera, work with lighting, and create stunning photos? Have you ever considered turning that energy and talent into a profitable business?

As a professional photographer, you can take pictures of people, places, and products for clients; sell your own personal photographs; and even teach others how to take pictures.

Education/Skills

Anyone with a camera can take a picture; and with smartphones being as popular as they are, millions of people are doing just that. But it takes more than a phone and an Instagram filter to make a professional photographer.

If you want to survive in this business, you need creativity, interpersonal skills, a good eye for detail, and the technical ability to work your camera and photo-editing software. You can easily develop your skills more economically through online tutorials, local classes and workshops, and good old-fashioned practice.

Realistic Expectations

Everyone needs a photographer at some point in their life — weddings, graduations, sporting events, parties, new babies — you name it. With the right talent and equipment, you can easily break into the market through family and friends. However, with thousands of potential clients out there, that means that there are even more competitors. Being able to market yourself will be the deciding factor in your success.

Making Bank

The average salary of a photographer is $16.15 an hour.[24]

Business Equipment

As a professional photographer, you will need a camera, lenses, filters, lighting equipment, a tripod, a powerful computer with photo-editing software, a photo printer, backgrounds, stools, and a studio.

Marketing Tips

Like we said, you probably have plenty of friends and family members who either need a photographer or know someone who does. Offer to be a second shooter at a wedding, and tell anyone you know that you are looking for clients and experience. You can also hand out business cards, put up posters, take out classified newspaper ads, and ask for referrals from customers and other people you know.

---

24. PayScale, 2017.

In this digital age, it's also important to develop a strong internet presence. As a photographer, you can do this through social media, personal blogs and websites, or online galleries like Behance and Flickr.

Additional Resources

www.photographyconcentrate.com

www.digital-photography-school.com

www.photographercentral.com

22.   Translator

Business Overview

Can you speak and write a different language fluently? Translators can work in both oral and written translation. Currently there are very few translators; therefore, this field is easy to break into.

Translate your language specialty into English, or vice-versa, in both oral and written form.

Education/Skills

A degree or background in the language(s) you are translating and good written and oral communication skills in both English and the language(s) are necessary.

Making Bank

The average salary of a translator is $19.84 an hour.[25]

Business Equipment

You might consider a pager if you intend on being on call with area firms, such as hospitals and courts, database software, and reference books, as well as the basic home-office equipment

Marketing Tips

If you are interested in working as a translator for area firms, contact them directly, leaving your name and contact information.

25. PayScale, 2017.

23. Email and Marketing Automation

Business Overview

Many businesses now automate their marketing process. You know those emails with ads from Target that you get all the time from a "Do Not Reply To" email address? You'd be helping with that. Sending out automated emails is just one part of the job — marketing automation entails getting information on users' IP addresses when they come to the company's website, monitors the website in other ways, etc.

Education/Skills

You'll need to be able to work with various computer programs. Sometimes you can't get a job without a marketing degree.

Realistic Expectations

What you'll most likely be doing is picking up side jobs for smaller companies. Some small business might want someone to put in marketing automation for their website.

Making Bank

The average salary of email and marketing automation is $20 an hour.[26]

Business Equipment

You'll need software, a reliable computer, and good Wi-Fi.

---

26. PayScale, 2017.

Marketing Tips

Learn as much as you can about the job by reading online articles. Contact businesses and keep applying for jobs on Upwork until you get something. Be persistent — it may take a lot of effort.

Additional Resources

www.blog.marketo.com/2012/11/what-is-the-difference-between -email-marketing-and-marketing-automation.html

24. Telemarketing and Telesales

Business Overview

As a telemarketer, you'll be generating interest in your product. As a tele-salesman or telesaleswoman, you'll be making sales, but all of it will be over the phone.

Education/Skills

This job often requires a high school diploma, but if you're willing to work and can prove your competency, you could get the job.

Realistic Expectations

Telemarketing and telesales are declining as a method for companies to generate sales — mostly because people don't talk on the phone as much as they used to. But the good news is that the jobs do indeed exist, and they don't require many qualifications, so you should have a shot at getting one.

Making Bank

The average salary of a telemarketer is $10.54 an hour.[27]

Business Equipment

The company will probably supply the phone — they'll have some kind of software to facilitate making calls — but you might have to supply a computer.

Marketing Tips

Remember, even though you have school during business hours, and most telemarketing or telesales calls are going to occur during business hours, you could always call people in a different time zone.

Additional Resources

www.virtual-sales.com/telemarketing-or-telesales/

25. SEO–Search Engine Optimization

Business Overview

Your goal is to make the websites of the businesses that you work for the most popular ones online. You want the website of the business to be the first Google result when someone searches related terms, and you'll do that by analyzing other website, employing keywords and links, and writing content.

---

27. PayScale, 2017.

Education/Skills

You can acquire a great deal of the knowledge needed without a formal degree; however, some businesses may prefer to hire people with a bachelor's degree.

Realistic Expectations

While there are many people trying to make money with this flexible and convenient job, there are also nearly countless options. Almost every business has a website.

Making Bank

The average salary of search engine optimization is $17.08 an hour.[28]

Business Equipment

You'll need a computer with good Wi-Fi.

Marketing Tips

Contact businesses and ask if they need an SEO freelancer for their website. Look on Upwork. The jobs are out there!

Additional Resources

www.locationrebel.com/seo-writing-for-beginners/

www.searchengineland.com/seo-simple-child-can-5-easy-steps -237473

---

28. PayScale, 2017.

26. Customer Service

Business Overview

Do you like interacting with people, but in your own space and way? Offering virtual customer service could be the right job for you!

According to www.**womenforhire.com**, many companies are now outsourcing customer service calls to "virtual agents."

Education/Skills

You will need to be good at multitasking and at speaking clearly and pleasantly. Many of the companies hiring virtual customer service representatives want candidates with at least a high school degree, but it's worth a try!

Realistic Expectations

There are a lot of offers out there for this kind of work. In fact, you have to be careful due to scams. There may be fewer opportunities that there initially seem to be because of this.

Making Bank

The average salary of customer service is $14.22 an hour.[29]

Business Equipment

You'll need a phone, a computer, and Wi-Fi. The company will of course give you guidelines on what kind of phone you'll need. It may have to be a landline phone, and you may have to pay for it (www.**womenforhire. com**).

Marketing Tips

You want to do your research so you can land a longer-term position at a company you like. See if anyone you know has ever done any job like this, and ask him or her for recommendations.

27.	E-book Producer/Publisher

Business Overview

Just about everyone has something they could teach someone else or a few tricks to improve the current way of doing something.

---

29. PayScale, 2017.

Your list of duties for putting together an e-book site could get pretty hefty. Some of your duties will include:

- Soliciting writers to submit their e-books

- Write e-books

- Read each submission

- Decide which books are best to be promoted (only about four or five each month in the beginning, until you get a feel for a schedule)

- Edit the e-books

- Promote the e-books

- Send out press releases

- Submit the e-book to critics for industry reviews

- Send out promotional advertisements

- Solicit for advertisement in the book

Education/Skills

A publishing background or an English degree would be highly recommended. If neither of these applies to you, you could pick up a class or workshop about the writing and publishing industry.

Making Bank

The average salary of an e-book publisher is $19.32 an hour.[30]

---

30. PayScale, 2017.

Business Equipment

E-book creator software, contracts for writers and illustrators, and, if you will be developing the website, web design and development software, with e-commerce development will be needed.

Marketing Tips

Learn what you can about the publishing and e-book industry. Take some industry crash courses or workshops to get a better understanding of the industry mechanics.

28.   Professional Researcher

Business Overview

Research can be a grueling and time consuming job, but research is not all you will need to do. Other duties include:

- Read and research information from periodicals, online, and through various other published works

- Write a report and detailed list of the information you obtained

- Write a report from audio tracks of information provided from the client or other sources

Other duties may be involved that include detailing your findings in an audio version or other multimedia format.

Education/Skills

Good oral communication and writing skills are a must, as well as an understanding of research, libraries, and how to obtain information.

Making Bank

The average salary of a professional researcher is $20 an hour.[31]

Business Equipment

Research software and database software, reference books, and other research information materials will be needed.

Marketing Tips

Find research jobs on job boards such as **www.upwork.com**.

29.   Illustrator

Business Overview

Can you draw and write funny captions? Can you create panel cartoons that get a laugh?

Provide pencil drawings with funny captions.

---

31. Glassdoor, 2017.

Education/Skills

You should understand cartoons and how they work and how to submit to newspapers and syndicates. This can be easily learned through books and periodicals.

Making Bank

The average salary of an illustrator is $20 an hour.

Business Equipment

An artist's table, drawing pencils, and drawing equipment are necessary, as well as the basic home office equipment.

Marketing Tips

Put together a syndication package as the syndicate you would like to be published with describes. Some syndication will be different, so adhere to the guidelines accordingly. The online links are companies who you can submit your column to, but most ask for about eight to ten cartoons at first, so make sure they are the best you have.

For self-syndication you will need to contact editors yourself with a query letter and offer the cartoon directly to them. This will eliminate the middle man (the syndicate) and bring you in direct contact with the editors. To find every newspaper worldwide with contact information, log onto **www.newslink.org**.

Chapter 4

Channel Your Creative Side

30. Fashion Designer

Business Overview

A fashion designer is someone who designs various aspects of fashion, typically clothes. Designers usually sketch out designs and then gather fabric to sew and make their creations and visions come to life.

Education/Skills

You don't necessarily have to have any education to design clothes; some people are just born with the natural talent. If you want, there are classes you can take that focus on how to design clothes and sketch designs.

Realistic Expectations

This can be a realistic career if you know people that are looking for clothes that they can't seem to find in stores. Commissions can also help you make more money.

Making Bank

The average salary of a fashion designer is $17.52 an hour.[32]

CASE STUDY: EMILY COSTA
Founder/Designer of Rebel Redefined,
21 years old
@emilycosta
@rebel_redefined
www.rebelredefined.com

Fashion has always been a huge interest of mine, and it's hard to think of a time when it wasn't! When I was younger, I found a real joy in dressing up and experimenting with my own individual style. For me, there was always something very unique and special in the ability to convey who I was as a person through my style.

Growing up, I always had an entrepreneurial spirit that really developed and took over while I was in high school. During those years, I dedicated myself to learning as much as I could about the fashion industry as a whole. I was consistently inspired by the idea of owning my own brand.

Two things really prepared me for this venture; one was attending Teen Vogue's Fashion University in New York City in 2011 for the first time at age 16. The other was taking a pre-college intensive course at the Fashion Institute of Technology in New York City on how to start and manage a small business. I used the knowledge I learned from successful designers like Michael Kors and Alexander Wang that spoke at Teen Vogue's Fashion U and the lessons I learned at FIT that summer and applied them to make my vision come to life.

I was 17 when I launched my brand Rebel Redefined. That same year, my brand was sold on NYLON magazines shop, featured in many articles, and worn by celebrities. I think my brand gained popularity so fast because it came from an authentic vision. People from all over the world really connected with the concept of the brand, which has always been fun, edgy, and a testament to being yourself.

I had to learn every aspect of running a business while preparing to launch. I did a lot of extensive research to figure out what would be the best ways to manage Rebel Redefined and the vision I had. I figured out how to design a website on my own, I contacted local printing shops to figure out how to manufacture our products, and I learned about marketing techniques to get the brand in the public eye. I read tons of books and articles online to make sure I understood what went into a successful business.

An important lesson I've learned is that there is a lot of trial and error — especially when first starting out. You have to see what works best for your vision and what will be the most effective! Truthfully, I still am learning every single day, but that is one of the joys of owning your own company. Every day is a new adventure, and you are forever growing as a designer and entrepreneur!

Business Equipment

You will need a sketchbook, a sewing machine, and various fabrics.

Marketing Tips

Think about making a site for yourself where people can look at clothes you've designed in the past. Also consider making an online store where people can purchase your designs. Make business cards so that if you're out and about and someone compliments your style, you can give them a business card.

Additional Resources

**www.cssauthor.com/75-beautiful-fashion-website-designs-for-your
-inspiration/**

31.   Event Planner

Business Overview

You will attend many special events in your life: birthday parties, weddings, baby showers, etc. Sometimes people don't know what they want, or they know exactly what they want but they can't afford it. It's the event planner's job to help these people find solutions to these problems. If you're creative, highly organized, detail-oriented, and can deal with demanding people, you might be a good fit for event planning.

Education/Skills

Many adults have spent a lot of hours training and going to school for jobs in the event planning field. The most important skills you'll need are organization, creativity, and communication, and you don't need to go to school to learn any of those things. Planning and organization are key skills because big events can be stressful and chaotic. Creativity is important because few people want a cookie-cutter event. Finally, good communication skills are vital because you'll be in charge of planning some of the biggest moments in people's lives, and everyone involved needs to know exactly what that entails.

Realistic Expectations

You'll have to start small, with events for friends and family. Perhaps begin by focusing on smaller events (like birthday parties) that don't have a lifetime of hopes and dreams riding on them and that will fit into your schedule if you're in school. Most of your events will happen on evenings and weekends, so understand that the hours are just part of the commitment to being your own boss. A good general rule for gaining customers is to dress like a professional.

Making Bank

The average salary of an event planner is $16.13 an hour.[33]

Business Equipment

This is a pretty cheap venture to start, as far as equipment goes. Bare-bones, you'll need a reliable vehicle, a camera, and some kind of note-taking system.

Marketing Tips

Once you've got some experience under your belt (no matter how small) get your name and business card out to local venues, florists, bakeries, musicians, and anybody else you can think of who would play a part in some kind of special event.

Additional Resources

www.eventplanningblueprint.com/your-10-steps-to-becoming-an
-event-planner/

www.wikihow.com/Become-an-Event-Planner

www.elearners.com/education-resources/degrees-and-programs/mini
-guide-to-a-wedding-planner-certification-online/

www.payscale.com/research/US/Job=Event_Coordinator/Salary/

---

33. PayScale, 2017.

32.   Floral Designer

Business Overview

If you enjoy working with flowers and plants, floral designer might be the job for you.

Education/Skills

There are no formal education requirements for floral design, though there are optional certification courses available. The most important innate skills you'll need are creativity, an eye for color and design, and some pretty green thumbs.

Realistic Expectations

This job will be more in demand during certain times of the year, like wedding season and around the major holidays. Be aware that this means longer hours during these times, so you'll just have to suck it up and buckle down.

Making Bank

The average salary of a floral designer is $12.61 an hour.[34]

Business Equipment

Walk into your local florist, or even your grocery store, and look at the equipment there: refrigeration units, a water supply, containers, ribbons, workstation, floral foam, and flowers.

Marketing Tips

Start building your reputation with family and friends. Once you've got some business cards, start meeting with local event venues, DJs, dress shops, and bakeries to get yourself into the market for larger events. Most importantly, make sure that everyone who sees one of your arrangements knows it came from you!

Additional Resources

www.bls.gov/ooh/arts-and-design/floral-designers.htm

www.theartcareerproject.com/becoming-a-floral-designer/

www.aifd.org/

---

34. PayScale, 2017.

33. Craft Show Organizer

Business Overview

As a craft show organizer you won't necessarily be dealing with one person's vision of an event. You may have a community or association of artists who seek your help in making their work more visible to the public. You may be working with a charity or a non-profit to raise money for their cause.

Education/Skills

There is no formal training required. Important skills here are organization, budgeting, creativity, and communication. Ultimately, your job is to show off other people's work in the best possible way, and that will take a lot of collaboration and teamwork.

Realistic Expectations

Think carefully about the kind of show you want to be known for hosting and the quality of the work you want to showcase. You will be responsible for advertising to promote your shows and each vendor, mapping out the space to be sure it won't get overcrowded, providing access to utilities for vendors, and providing tables and chairs. Some venues may be able to help you with some of these things, so don't be afraid to ask!

Making Bank

The average salary of a craft show organizer is $17 an hour.[35]

---

35. PayScale, 2017.

Business Equipment

You will need access to email. If venues can't provide tables and chairs, you may have to invest in them.

Marketing Tips

Choose dates for your shows and stick with them year after year. Eventually they'll make their way into the public consciousness, and customers will look forward to your shows each year. Build yourself a website to keep the public updated on your events, and be sure to include a small profile for each artist you will be featuring, with links to their own websites or social media pages.

Additional Resources

www.entrepreneur.com/businessideas/craft-shows www.askharriete .typepad.com/ask_harriete/2012/12/responsibilities-of-craft-show -organizers.html www.mnartists.org/article/confessions-craft-show -organizer

34. Gift Basket / Crate Designer

Business Overview

There are baskets full of makeup, perfume, and nail polish; crates full of razors, shaving soap, and cologne. They make them for men, women, children, and even pets! If you're creative and you like giving unique gifts, you can grab a slice of this booming business for yourself.

Education/Skills

There are online video-based courses taught by professional gift basket designers, or books you could purchase and study.

Realistic Expectations

The benefits to this type of business are numerous. You'll get to exercise your creativity by building a new collection of themed items every so often. Once people subscribe, you'll have capital to work with, creating a steady stream of income.

Making Bank

The average salary of a gift basket designer is $11.84 an hour.[36]

Business Equipment

You may want to maintain an inventory of baskets, boxes, and other containers; decorative filler; assorted ribbons and bows; and cellophane shrink wrap.

Marketing Tips

Depending on the type of business you're interested in, try to find similar companies and research their marketing practices. Approach local artists and craftspeople about featuring their items in your collections. Offer to expand their markets in exchange for bulk purchasing at lower cost to you. Use branded stickers and packaging whenever possible.

---

36. PayScale, 2017.

Additional Resources

www.entrepreneur.com/article/37926

www.giftbasketbusinessworld.com/resources/classes/

www.smallbusiness.chron.com/start-gift-basket-business-monthly
-fees-4626.html

hwww.giftbasketstatistics.com/

35. Interior Decorator

Business Overview

Have the words "rustic" and "chic" become major parts of your vocabulary? Can you turn a cheap wooden pallet into something other than a collection of splinters and an infection? The cure may be to go into business as an interior decorator.

Education/Skills

You cannot become an interior designer without at least an associate's degree, so that's off-limits to you as a teen. However, there is no such requirement for being a decorator.

Realistic Expectations

One way to set yourself apart is with your sense of style. If you're doing something that nobody else is doing, that could attract business, but don't get too crazy. Your market determines the business you get, so look carefully at the design trends in your area.

Making Bank

The average salary of an interior decorator is $20.26 an hour.[37]

Business Equipment

You may want to invest in some specialty interior design software. A reliable vehicle to get you around town is important. Order collections of fabric swatches and paint samples.

Marketing Tips

Offer free consultations and perhaps a discount to current customers for referring a friend. Get references whenever possible, and use them in your brochure and on your website.

Additional Resources

**www.payscale.com/research/US/Job=Interior_Decorator/Hourly
_Rate**

**www.study.com/articles/Become_a_Certified_Interior_Decorator
_CID_Step-by-Step_Guide.html**

**www.freshome.com/2009/02/10/how-to-become-an-interior
-decorator/**

www.wikihow.com/Become-an-Interior-Decorator

---

37. PayScale, 2017.

36. Disc Jockey

Business Overview

When you're a disc jockey, the party never starts without you. DJs introduce and play recorded music for all sorts of occasions — birthday parties, charity events, weddings, festivals, community events, and dance clubs.

Education/Skills

While there are no formal requirements needed to be a DJ, the job still requires a lot of skill. All good DJs need a passion for music, good communication skills, an outgoing personality, the ability to read a crowd, knowledge of music history and popular songs, and the know-how to operate their computer and sound equipment.

Realistic Expectations

This is a fairly competitive market, but it can be a great way to earn money once you have built up some experience and connections.

Making Bank

The average salary of a disc jockey is $40.96 an hour.

Business Equipment

DJs are responsible for providing their own audio equipment — such as speakers, subwoofers, turntables, mixers, microphones, karaoke machines, and a collection of licensed music.

Marketing Tips:

Start your own website and announce your services on social media. As you build up your business, hand out business cards.

Additional Resources

www.djtimes.com

www.adja.org

www.promobiledj.com

37. Scrapbooker

Business Overview

We want to provide context for the photos we've taken so that we, and maybe future generations of our families, can enjoy looking back on the important moments in our history. Some of us might be good at doing this ourselves, but many of us aren't.

Education/Skills

People you work for will have different tastes and ideas, so if you have the ability to adapt to their style, you will go far in this business.

Realistic Expectations

You will want to keep up with the trends and any new equipment that comes on the market. The most difficult parts of this job will be finding customers and amassing an inventory of supplies.

Making Bank

The average salary of a scrapbooker is $9 an hour.[38]

Business Equipment

First and foremost, you will need a computer and a high-quality combination printer and scanner. Photo-editing software may come in handy if you're dealing with older photos or photos that were damaged in some way. Purchase the items that will be useful on every single project.

---

38. Glassdoor, 2017.

Marketing Tips

Start by making your own scrapbook and some individual pages for your friends and family. Build a physical and online portfolio of your best work. Make your own business cards, and try to make them stand out from the standard ones you see everywhere.

Additional Resources

www.frugalmom.net/scrapbooking_business.htm

38.   Picture Framer

Business Overview

If you love art so much that you'd risk going to museum jail and you're interested in protecting it for future generations of lawbreakers, you should consider becoming a custom picture framer.

Education/Skills

You don't need to take any classes to become a framer, though classes do exist. It is possible to teach yourself with the right information, tools, and lots of practice. The Professional Picture Framers Association is a great resource for both aspiring and successful framers.

Realistic Expectations

Some people don't know what they like, or can't explain it, or they ask for your opinion and then immediately torpedo your ideas. You'll have to learn to read your customers well, to know when to lead and when to follow.

Making Bank

The average salary of a picture framer is $12.11 an hour.[39]

Business Equipment

This job does require some significant startup investment, but it also depends on what kind of framer you want to be. You can go full-bore and order computerized mat cutters and design systems, and keep stock of every mat board, frame style, and glazing on the market. On the other hand, you could get a simple manual mat cutter and samples of the frames, boards, and glazing to show customers.

Marketing Tips

Take photos of your best work (with permission from customers) for your portfolio. Many people don't recognize the value of custom framing until they're shown the difference between pre-made products and high-quality custom ones.

Additional Resources

www.ppfa.com/

www.logangraphic.com/the-complete-guide-to-the-picture-framing -process/ www.pictureframingmagazine.net/

www.payscale.com/research/US/Job=Framer_-_Art,_Mirrors, _Pictures/Hourly_Rate

---

39. PayScale, 2017.

39.   Costume Designer

Business Overview

Costumes designers make costumes for various types of production whether that be for a play or musical. Designers can even make costumes for various things like Halloween.

Education/Skills

You don't necessarily have to have any education to design costumes; some people are just born with the natural talent. If you want, there are classes you can take that focus on how to design costumes.

Realistic Expectations

This can be a realistic career if you know people that are looking for costumes that they can't seem to find in stores.

Making Bank

The average salary of a costume designer is $17.62 an hour.[40]

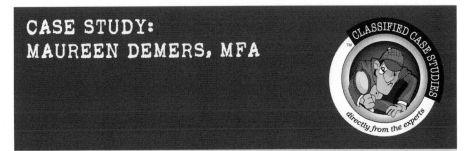

CASE STUDY:
MAUREEN DEMERS, MFA

Maureen (Molly) Demers "fell madly in love" with costume design while in college to earn her theater degree.

"It's exciting; it changes all the time," she says of her job as a community theater costume designer. "I like to build and create. I love historical replication."

Molly encourages students interested in costume design to consider a theater degree rather than focusing only on fashion design. "Try every area of theater," she says. "You will be more successful if you understand the other areas like acting, directing, set design and lighting. If you are well-rounded and knowledgeable, you understand what the actors and director need from you, and you can do your job more collaboratively with everyone else."

Molly recommends students get experience by volunteering with a school or community theater and says a young person can even learn a lot about fabrics and all the pieces involved by working at a fabric store.

---

40. Bureau of Labor Statistics, 2016.

Business Equipment

You will need a sketchbook, a sewing machine, and various fabrics.

Marketing Tips

Think about making a site for yourself where people can look at clothes you've designed in the past. Also consider making an online store where people can purchase your designs. Make business cards to hand out during opportune times like Halloween.

Additional Resources

www.costumepage.org/tcpmake2.html

www.coolest-homemade-costumes.com/making-halloween-costumes .html

www.cadcam.solutionsaustralia.com.au/Costumes.htm

40.   Music Lessons

Business Overview

As a music teacher, you will work with a class or one on one with private students to teach them how to play an instrument.

Education/Skills

The best music teachers know the basics of music theory, can read music, teach students how to read music, and identify their students' skill level and tailor lesson plans for them.

Realistic Expectations

Getting a music teaching studio off the ground can be hard work, but it's possible if you advertise your services, charge what you're worth, and teach a popular instrument.

Making Bank

The average salary of a music teacher is $45 an hour.[41]

Business Equipment

Equipment will vary depending on the instrument you teach. You may need a spare instrument, music books, notebooks, pencils, and pens.

Marketing Tips

Post fliers in community centers, libraries, school bulletin boards, and other places where families and students will see them. Create your own blog or website, put ads in your local newspaper, ask for referrals from friends and family members, announce your new business on social media, and take advantage of tutoring sites like **www.TakeLessons.com** and **www. Care.com.**

Additional Resources

www.musiclessonsresource.com

www.blog.musicteachershelper.com

www.wyzant.com

---

41. PayScale, 2017.

41.　Painter (Artist)

Business Overview

As a painter, you can create and sell your artwork, take requests from clients, as well as coach others how to paint.

Education/Skills

While it's true that anyone with a paintbrush can paint, you need artistic ability, business acumen, and interpersonal skills to make the most out of this business.

Realistic Expectations

The starving artist is a cliché for a reason. The market is not only saturated with gifted painters starting their own businesses, but clients can be very hard to find. Still, when talent is mixed with dedication and good business skills, there are plenty of ways to break into the industry and earn money.

Making Bank

The average salary of a painter is $16.22 an hour.[42]

Business Equipment

Some common tools include paints, brushes, painting surfaces, easels, towels, water, and varnish. If you want to sell your work online, you will also need a camera, a computer, and an internet connection.

---

42. PayScale, 2017.

Marketing Tips

In the digital era, developing a strong internet presence is essential for any business. As an artist, you can do this through social media, through a personal blog or website, or through online galleries like ARTmine. You can also market yourself by entering art competitions, submitting applications to art galleries, selling your paintings at community events, donating some of your work to charities, networking with other artists, and putting your paintings on sites like eBay and Etsy.

Additional Resources

www.art-mine.com

www.emptyeasel.com

www.theartcareerproject.com/5-tips-to-building-your-own-art -business

Chapter 5

DIY Junkies Unite!

42. Upcycling

Business Overview

They say that one man's trash is another man's treasure; when it comes to upcycling, the saying couldn't be truer. Upcycling is when you take old or discarded items and create something of greater value. It's is a fantastic way to exercise your creativity while also caring for the environment and making money.

Education/Skills

There are no educational requirements in this business. When it comes to upcycling, all you need is a little business acumen, some artistic flair, a knack for finding the potential in old items, and the ability to accomplish your vision.

Realistic Expectations

No matter where you live, there is likely a wealth of free and cheap items to be found for upcycling. If you can turn this material into interesting pieces that people want to buy, then you've got an excellent chance of getting your business off the ground. All it takes is time, talent, and dedication.

Making Bank

When calculating how much to charge for a certain piece, consider the original cost of the item and your materials, as well as the time you spent upcycling it.

Business Equipment

Some common tools include paint, fabric, screwdrivers, hammers, paintbrushes, glue, scissors, pliers, staple guns, and sandpaper. You will also want a camera and a computer if you want to sell or advertise your items online.

Marketing Tips

When you first start out, let your friends and family know that you are starting an upcycling business. This can be done in person or on social media and will generate interest in your products. Start a blog and post pictures of the items you've refurbished, and see if anyone you know is interested in buying them.

Additional Resources

www.freecycle.org

www.artfire.com

www.hipcycle.com

43. Jewelry Designer

Business Overview

Do you love jewelry but hate seeing the same kind of items everywhere you go? Have you purchased a piece only to find that it turned your skin a gangrenous shade of green? If you're the world's next Pandora, Swarovski, or Alex & Ani, you could make a killing in the jewelry design business.

Education/Skills

If you're driven enough to do the studying on your own, there are hundreds of books available to you that will teach you everything from basic skills to advanced techniques. Jewelry design requires a lot of hands-on work, so taking a few classes at your local craft store can familiarize you with the tools of the trade, and give you an idea of what you like to make. You will need to be creative, tenacious, and good with your hands.

Realistic Expectations

First step: find a niche you'd like to occupy. Whatever specialty you choose, familiarize yourself with the tools, raw materials, and processes that are necessary and common within it. When you've mastered those, move on to more advanced techniques, and practice everything until you could do it in your sleep.

Making Bank

The average salary of a jewelry designer is $19 an hour.[43]

---

43. PayScale, 2017.

Business Equipment

Depending on your niche you may need an inventory of beads or stones in every color of the rainbow, a torch and lampworking supplies, soldering irons and metalworking tools, etc. You'll also need storage cases to keep all this stuff organized and display racks to show off your work.

Marketing Tips

Word-of-mouth really is the best advertising you could get. Make jewelry for people you know who will wear it prominently out in public. Rent a booth at craft fair or farmer's markets. Design branded cards for earring display and branded tags for other items. Take pictures of all your designs and start building a portfolio.

Additional Resources

www.theartcareerproject.com/become-jewelry-designer/

www.wikihow.com/Become-a-Jewelry-Designer

www.payscale.com/research/US/Job=Jewelry_Designer/Salary

44. Candle making

Business Overview

Everyone loves candles. With the strike of a match, a well-placed candle can bring a cozy aura to any room, and a scented candle can make your house smell like fresh cookies or sheets without the hassle of baking or cleaning.

Education/Skills

There are plenty of tutorials and videos to be found online that break down what kind of wax, wicks, and containers to use, along with other techniques of the trade. And if you think you need more hands-on training, check around your community to see if any craft stores, gift shops, or community colleges offer classes.

Realistic Expectations

If you can get your product into local or online stores, you will likely make a few sales. It will take a good candle and a special niche — as well as creative branding and advertising — to make a more than a supplemental income in this business.

Making Bank

The average salary of a candle maker is $15 an hour.[44]

Business Equipment

Common items for candle making include wax, wicks, containers, fragrance oils, dyes, molds, saucepans, labels, a scale, a thermometer, and a heat source. Additionally, complete candle-making kits can be found online and in certain craft stores. If you plan to sell your candles online, a computer and camera will also come in handy.

Marketing Tips

The best way to sell candles is to identify an audience and then mold your product to them.

When you have your candles ready and your audience in mind, it's time to start selling. To sell online, you can use stores like eBay or Etsy, or you can create your own personal website. To sell your candles locally, visit gift shops in your area and see if they are interested in selling your product. Also, stay active on social media to keep your customers interested and engaged.

Additional Resources

www.candles.org

www.etsy.com

www.candlewic.com

---

44. Economic Research Institute, Inc.,2017.

45. Seamstress/Tailor

Business Overview

While this profession does require highly-skilled and disciplined individuals, it's also a kind of art. Sewing professionals help their customers achieve a level of confidence that would be hard to find while wearing ill-fitting, off-the-rack clothing. If you love fashion and want to make people feel good, seamstress/tailor might be the right career path for you.

Education/Skills

An attention to detail, good hand-eye coordination, math skills, some mechanical aptitude, and problem solving are all important to the production side of the business. On the management side, the ability to work within a budget and good organizational and communication skills will be helpful.

Realistic Expectations

There are hundreds of textbooks available to help you, but hands-on training is important as well. If your local craft store offers beginner sewing classes, take them! There is specialized equipment you will need to use and (possibly) repair. Buy bargain-bin fabric to practice on until you're comfortable with your machines and what they can do. Try altering some clothing to fit you or a friend.

Making Bank

The average salary of a tailor is $15.38 an hour.[45]

---

45. PayScale, 2017.

Business Equipment

The first thing you will need is a standard sewing machine. At the bare minimum you will need a mannequin or two, needles (for the machine and for hand-sewing), bobbins, thread, fabric, linings, fasteners of all types, a measuring tape, a fabric-marking pencil, pins, a pincushion, and high-quality fabric shears in several sizes. Don't forget to buy hangers, garment bags and boxes, and tissue paper for when your customers pick up their purchases.

Marketing Tips

Word-of-mouth is the best kind of advertising, so clothe as many people as you can to start spreading the word. If there are fashion designers in your area, partner with them to do last-minute alterations for their fashion shows. Help out your local theater company by sewing or altering costumes for their next production in exchange for advertising.

Additional Resources

www.study.com/articles/How_to_Become_a_Professional_Seamstress _Education_and_Career_Roadmap.html

www.learn.org/articles/Seamstress_5_Steps_to_Becoming_a _Seamstress.html

www.sewingprofessionals.org/certification-program

46. Potter

Business Overview

I thought Daniel Radcliffe had this nailed down already, but if you really want to be the next "Boy Who Lived," who am I to crush your dreams? Oh wait . . . not *the* Potter; a person who makes things out of clay for a living? Okay cool, that's totally achievable.

Education/Skills

The most important skills here are attention to detail and physical strength. Success may be easier to find as a potter who makes practical things that people use every day. You'll need to be strong enough to lift heavy bags of clay or buckets of glaze and to center large pieces of clay on a wheel.

Realistic Expectations

You'll have to learn how to manhandle heavy balls of clay so they don't fly off the wheel like a shot-put when you turn it on. Strength is important but so is leverage, and learning how to use your weight as a tool to provide constant, even pressure will save your muscles from overuse. Find a class or a workshop to attend that will show you the basics and allow you to familiarize yourself with the equipment and the process. Pottery is an expensive undertaking, and you don't want to be purchasing equipment you don't need or can't operate.

Making Bank

The average salary of a potter is $23.45 an hour.[46]

Business Equipment

There are too many methods to explain in detail here, so take some classes and start studying to find the path that's right for you. No matter what method you choose, there are some things you will need: clay, sculpting tools, buckets, sponges, glazes, paintbrushes, and a workspace with storage and running water. Don't forget craft paper for wrapping finished pieces when they are sold or put into storage, and gift bags or boxes for sales.

Marketing Tips

Get yourself a booth at local craft shows or farmers' markets to show off your work to the community. Approach local galleries about hosting a show if your pottery is more artistic than functional. Get some stickers

---

46. Bureau of Labor Statistics, 2016.

printed with your company name and logo to put on bags or boxes when you sell items.

Additional Resources

www.ceramicartsdaily.org/ceramic-art-and-artists/ceramic-artists /4-successful-potters-give-advice-on-how-to-make-a-living-making -pottery/

www.craftcouncil.org/post/eat-pay-love-potters-business-model

www.theartcareerproject.com/ceramics/803/

47. Creating Homemade Skin-Care and Grooming Products

Business Overview

Homemade natural beauty and grooming products are a booming business, and you could get in on this trend with just a little time and effort.

Education/Skills

No formal training is required, but an interest in science is a good place to start. Even if you're using someone else's basic recipes, you're responsible for selling safe products, so learning some basic biology about human skin and hair will be helpful. Most people like their products to smell nice, so a functional sense of smell will be useful as well.

Realistic Expectations

Research similar businesses in your area and look for a niche that's not being filled. Maybe your competition focuses mainly on lotion and soap, leaving the scrub and mask niche wide open. Perhaps you can take advantage of two trends at once and create a line of mustache waxes and beard oils. Whatever the gap, make it your own, even if it's not the thing you were originally intending to focus on.

Making Bank

It might be tricky to first starting getting customers but once you get customers who love your product you can continue to thrive! Create special promotions so that people will want to buy even more of your product. Think of promotions like 20 percent off sales or buy one, get one sales! These sales will also help your customers continue to spread the news about your wonderful products!

Business Equipment

You should be able to find your own glass bowls, measuring spoons and cups, spoons for stirring, a scale, a thermometer, and a handheld mixer for very little money. Some products might require heat, so a microwave or portable electric burner could be necessary. Try to find bulk versions of basic ingredients, like sugar and beeswax to save money, and store items in the manner recommended by their manufacturers. Hard soaps require molds, and you'll need jars of all sizes for liquid products. When you sell items, you'll need branded packaging

Marketing Tips

Rent a booth at local craft shows and farmers' markets to showcase your wares. When you start building a customer base, get testimonials or reviews from your regulars to use in your marketing materials. Approach local gift shops, salons and day spas, and barber shops about selling your products if it suits their clientele.

Additional Resources

www.bulkapothecary.com

www.fromnaturewithlove.com/reprint/inhomeskincarebusiness.asp

www.theecologist.org/green_green_living/health_and_beauty /283760/how_to_make_your_own_skincare_products.html

www.handmadecosmeticallance.org/

48. Creating a Makeup Line

Business Overview

There are a lot of similarities between this job and the previous one, but caring for your hair and skin isn't the same thing as wearing makeup. If you're obsessed with finding beauty hacks on Pinterest, or following celebrity Instagram accounts for the latest trends, you could find some money and pleasure making your own beauty makeup at home.

Education/Skills

Some scientific aptitude could be helpful, and some knowledge of basic biology. A good eye for color will be important for this too, since your goal is to create products that make people look healthier, not sicklier.

Realistic Expectations

Let's look at beauty makeup first: It could be tough making a dent in the commercial beauty makeup business with all the products that are already out there. Another hurdle you may face is that many women are fiercely loyal to products they've been using their whole lives. Getting them to switch to a new and untested product could be incredibly difficult. Make samples for your friends and family to test, and welcome their honest opinions. The market for special effects makeup will be vastly different from the beauty makeup market, but different can be good. Of course, Halloween will be a busy time of year for you, and your demographic will include more men than it would for beauty makeup. If you live in an artsy community with a lot of theater programs, you could forge some great business relationships there.

Making Bank

The average salary of a makeup artist is $17.25 an hour.[47]

CASE STUDY: ZANDRA CUNNIGHAM

Zandra Cunningham
ZANDRA
Buffalo, NY
www.zandrabeauty.com

When did you start your business?

2009, I was nine years old.

I have always had a strong passion for lip balm/gloss. I would ask my dad every day before he went to work to bring me home a new lip balm. Finally, he told me NO and told me I should make my own! The rest is HISTORY!

What I like most about running my business is that I can use it as a vehicle for change. With me running my own business, I inspire others; both young and old to do the same; I love that!

Our gross profit margin is very good, and our sales are steadily increasing every year.

---

47. PayScale, 2017.

I operate my business inside my production studio that I have off-site. I have satisfactory equipment to currently meet the demands from our customers; however, I see a need for an upgrade to occur really soon. My parents and my younger brother work for me. I sometimes have my uncle and aunt work for me seasonally. Also, some of my friends will come in to help out/hang out.

For years it was very tough juggle work and school; with the last two years being the most challenging. Since the business is rising rapidly, we have decided that I will participate in homeschooling. By doing so, I can focus more on running my business while meeting the demands of school on my time, except my dad is a tough teacher!

The biggest sacrifice I have made is losing sleep. Although I don't get to hang out with my friends a lot; especially spontaneously, I really miss out on some valuable sleep.

My most satisfying moment as a business owner is being able to give back to girls' education. I really enjoy being able to help empower girls to follow their dreams

My parents help me out a lot. Not just with helping to finance my business, but constant encouragement and motivation. The fact that my parents are proud of me helps me to deal with sacrifices. My mom is my right hand, she is my mom-a-ger and she makes sure my scheduling is on task. My dad is my CFO, —he handles all of our numbers—and my teacher for homeschooling.

Dream BIG, Write a Plan, Follow the Plan, and Plan to have fun! I also want others to know that success comes with great sacrifice and hard work, but going through the pain, makes the success that much more gratifying.

Business Equipment

Get some glass bowls, measuring spoons and cups, a scale, a thermometer, spoons for stirring, and a handheld mixer. A microwave or portable electric burner could be necessary for products that need to be heated, and a small refrigerator for things that need to be cooled. Try to find bulk versions of basic ingredients to save money, and store items in the manner recommended by their manufacturers. You can purchase molds and packaging necessities from Bulk Apothecary, Making Cosmetics, or even Amazon. You'll need branded packaging for sales.

Marketing Tips

Craft shows and farmers' markets can give you some exposure in the community. Get reviews and testimonials from customers whenever possible. Beauty makeup can be sold in local gift shops or salons, and you could partner with fashion designers to do makeup for their shows. Special effects makeup will probably sell better online, but reach out to theme parks or haunted house attractions in your area for business opportunities. Use social media to showcase looks that were achieved with your products.

Additional Resources

www.leaf.tv/articles/how-to-make-your-own-makeup-at-home/

www.makingcosmetics.com/

www.makeuptutorials.com/22-diy-cosmetics-easy-makeup-recipe -ideas/

www.ehow.com/how_6629065_homemade-special-effects-makeup.html

www.instructables.com/id/Homemade-FX-Makeup/

www.work.chron.com/yearly-salary-makeup-artist-4856.html

49.   Crafting Scented Wax Tarts for Burners

Business Overview

You know how some smells can bring a memory rushing back to you? Maybe it's the smell of baking cookies in your mom's kitchen, or sawdust in your grandfather's workshop. You can bring memories to life by creating scented wax tarts for those popular wax burners.

Education/Skills

A healthy amount of caution in the presence of melted wax and a functional sense of smell. That is all. You just have to want to make things smell nice. Who isn't interested in that?

Realistic Expectations

Startup cost is very low, you won't need to spend a lot of time studying anything, and in the space of one afternoon you could have a reasonable amount of product ready for sale. Other than the occasional wax spill, the one thing you should be aware of is that you will smell like a candle factory at the end of the day.

Making Bank

The average salary for a craft artist is $18.70 an hour.[48]

Business Equipment

Hardware: Measuring cups and spoons, bowls, a scale, and a thermometer. An electric burner, pots, a spacious work surface, molds, and storage space. Software: Lots and lots of wax, colored dyes, and scented oils. Don't forget branded packaging supplies!

---

48. Bureau of Labor Statistics, 2016.

Marketing Tips

Craft shows, farmers' markets, and local gift shops will be good retail options for you. Local salons or day spas may be interested in purchasing certain scents from you to add to their ambiance.

Additional Resources

www.candletech.com/fragrant-living/make-wax-melt-tart-cubes/

www.instructables.com/id/Homemade-Scented-Wax-Melts/

50.   Reupholstering/Refinishing Furniture

Business Overview

If you like the idea of giving old things a new lease on life, you could start your own furniture refinishing business in your spare time.

Education/Skills

You will need attention to detail, good hand-eye coordination, and organizational and communication skills. You will also need to know how to use the tools of the trade, which will include hand and power tools, fabric, and chemical strippers and varnish. Being safe is always important. A willingness to follow health and safety rules will allow you to run your business for as long as you want without getting sidetracked by either a physical injury or brain damage caused by inhaling harsh chemicals. You may find upholstery classes through a local trade school or an adult education program. Take them if you can, or volunteer to help out at a local shop

Realistic Expectations

Start with refinishing furniture, since you can purchase how-to books from your local hardware store. Buy cheaply priced furniture from thrift stores to practice on. You can only refinish real wood, so look closely at your purchases. Take before and after photos of every project to show off in your marketing materials. Do small upholstery projects, like recovering a chair pad or re-stuffing couch cushions, and work your way up to more complicated projects. Doing small projects for friends or retail sale will teach you how to manage your time, and how to estimate your labor time and costs for future projects.

Making Bank

The average salary for reupholstering is $15.31 an hour.[49]

Business Equipment

For upholstery: an industrial sewing machine, an air-powered or electric stapler, measuring tools, and hand tools and power tools of all types and sizes. For a comprehensive list, visit **www.upholsteryresource.com/node /112**. For refinishing: an assortment of scrapers, hammers, and measuring tools; paintbrushes, paint trays, and painter's tape; and a respirator. For a complete list of necessary tools, visit "A Guide to Furniture Restoration Tools" on the *How Stuff Works* website.

Marketing Tips

Refinish your own furniture, or do small projects for friends to build up your portfolio and experience. This is another business where word-of-

---

49. PayScale, 2017.

mouth will be your greatest advertising tool. Get references and testimonials from customers as soon as you can. Make friends at the local thrift stores who can tell you when an interesting piece of furniture comes in. Partner with interior decorators or designers in your area whenever possible.

Additional Resources

www.upholsteryresource.com/

www.kimsupholstery.com/diy/5-secrets-running-successful-upholstery -business/

www.entrepreneur.com/businessideas/furniture-upholstery-service

www.home.howstuffworks.com/home-improvement/home-diy /furniture-restoration/a-guide-to-wooden-furniture-restoration-tools -ga.htm

www.payscale.com/research/US/Job=Upholsterer/Hourly_Rate

51. Creating Cards (Birthday, Wedding, Baby, etc.)

Business Overview

People need greeting cards for all sorts of occasions and events — birthdays, babies, anniversaries, marriages, graduations, and countless holidays like Mother's and Father's Day. It's no wonder that the American greeting card industry is priced at $7 billion.

As a greeting card creator, you will not only design and create cards, but you will explore the marketplace and find the best way to sell them to your customers.

Education/Skills

There are no educational requirements in this business. Artistic and business backgrounds are a plus; but if you can make greeting cards, then you can sell greeting cards.

Realistic Expectations

If you want make it as a new greeting card creator, you will have to create a product that sets you apart from the popular brands. With hard work, a well-advertised product, and the help of local and online stores, you can turn greeting cards into a profitable business.

Making Bank

The average salary of a greeting card designer is $22.33 an hour.[50]

Business Equipment

The materials and equipment you need to produce your cards will depend on the type of cards you create. Some common items include scissors, paper, cardstock, rice paper, ribbons, buttons, paint, pens, pencils, envelopes, a computer, photo editing software, and a high-quality printer.

Marketing Tips

To sell your product, two things have to happen: you need to know your audience and your audience needs to know you exist. Nail down a specific niche for your brand.

---

50. Study, 2017.

If you want to sell cards online, you can use online stores like eBay or Etsy, or you can create your own personal website. To sell your cards locally, visit gift shops and party supply stores in your area and see if they are interested in buying from you. Also, stay active on social media to keep your customers interested and engaged.

Additional Resources

www.rubberstamping.about.com

www.greetingcardassociation.org.uk

www.etsy.com

52.   Coffee Mug Designer

Business Overview

Do you have a knack for making creative designs? Do you have an eye for what would look good on a coffee mug to make a unique gift? Being a coffee mug designer could be the right job for you!

Education/Skills

You don't really need any special education for this job, but some basic familiarity with graphic design will be helpful. You'll need to make sure that the image looks good from every angle and that it doesn't get blurry on the final product.

Realistic Expectations

It isn't too hard to get into this industry — all you have to do is set up an account on websites like Zazzle, Cafepress, or Amazon. The first two sites take care of the processing and shipping — a big benefit for you!

Zazzle.com offers the opportunity to set up a free designer shop online. You can set the royalties at whatever you want (from 5% to 99%), but remember that if the product seems overpriced, fewer people might buy it. You might be better off with a lower royalty at first while you see how successful the product is.

Cafepress gives you multiple options on how to sell your product.

- You can sell for free in their online marketplace.

- You can pay $5 to $10 a month to set up your own online shop.

- You can do a crowdfunding campaign via the platform that Cafepress runs, Tfund. You set a goal on how much money you want to earn, and then you spread the word via social media.

- Amazon or Ebay might be better options if you want to hand paint or hand letter your mug. You can set up an account as a seller, but of course you will be in charge of shipping costs.

Making Bank

If you pay attention to customer trends — look on Amazon and see what kinds of items seem popular at certain times of year — you can probably make several thousand dollars a year with this easy, convenient side job. If you love graphic design and entrepreneurship, this job could help you put more money in your pocket.

Business Equipment

With a computer and some good Wi-Fi, you can operate your business from the comfort of your own room — or anywhere else. Photoshop and other basic graphic design software is really the only other equipment you'll need.

Marketing Tips

The real challenge with this business, as mentioned, is the difficulty of name recognition. What makes your little online shop different from hundreds of other online shops? How can you get anyone to recognize or know about you? Some ideas include establishing a blog with links to your Zazzle shop, for instance; spreading the word on social media; and even putting advertisements in local shops that are willing to work with you.

Chapter 6

If You're a People Person

53.   Lounge Owner

Business Overview

Are you dissatisfied with the current places to hang out and relax in your hometown? What if a shop for tea parties or an ice cream store with lots of comfy seating would fill a niche? And maybe you can be the person who fills that niche! You don't simply want to work for someone who own and operates his or her own lounge — you want to set the vision and tone for an entirely new place.

Education/Skills

If you're under 18, signing a five-year lease for a storefront may be next to impossible. The good news, however, is that no degrees, special courses, or licenses are required — of course, if you're serving food, the health department will have to license your business, but you personally don't need any additional training if you can drum up the money to rent a space and pay for the costs of producing your product.

Realistic Expectations

Teens who own their own lounges are a rarity — far less common than teens who babysit or watch their neighbors' dogs. So expect some difficulties — and even disbelief — when you talk to other people about your plan. Nevertheless, it has been done by teens before, even though you'll probably need monetary assistance from your parents and/or other sources. Don't lose hope!

Making Bank

The average salary of a restaurant owner is $20.86 an hour.[51]

CASE STUDY: NICO GIULIANTI

In 2014, I started on the business plan at 16-years-old. I opened it in 2016 at 18-years-old and a senior in high school.

Every time I travel, I find the area's local comic and game store; reading comics and graphic novels, as well as collecting related merchandise, is one of my passions. I noticed that my area — home to almost two million people — didn't have one in the downtown area where we lived. Even more importantly, I always felt rushed at the typical comic shop, unable to really relax and check out the whole selection. What if a comic store was really a "comics lounge" — a place where you could grab a coffee or bubble tea (my favorite) and sit and read a comic or play a game with your friends? I put the idea together for my father, a lawyer, and my mother, a bubble tea aficionado. They loved the idea, and then I sketched out the basic idea for the look and feel of the store.

51. PayScale, 2017.

Although the concept, business plan, and set up was my idea, I still have to finish high school, so I don't run the day-to-day operations. We hired a store manager to handle that, while I oversee what I love — marketing, advertising, and spreading the word about our unique comics lounge!

Comics and toys are a low profit margin business, but by adding the coffee and bubble tea bar we were able to quickly break even and are continuing to grow as word spreads.

Juggling my life and responsibilities has been very challenging. During weekdays I am typically at school, including on the bus, from 6:45 a.m. until 4:15 p.m. — nine and a half hours. Once I get home, I have a couple hours of homework, plus tutoring twice per week. Finally, before going to sleep, I spend time researching new products and creating new strategies for marketing the store.

My most satisfying moment was when we were a few days before opening, still receiving product and deciding placement for all the comics and merchandise, and a customer knocked on the door and asked to come in. Even though we weren't open, he came in and purchased two expensive superhero statues — and became my first customer!

I have three key pieces of advice for other teen entrepreneurs. First, research your idea and write the most detailed business plan you can. Figure out who your market is and what they want — not just what you want to sell them. Second, find a niche that isn't being filled in your area. For me, a comic book-bubble tea lounge was a unique offering not found anywhere. Third, make sure it's something you know and care about. My love for comics and graphic novels made starting such a store a natural idea.

Nico Giulianti owns Lauderdale Comics (www.lauderdalecomics.com) in Fort Lauderdale, Florida.

Business Equipment

You will need a lot of equipment — and the type of equipment will vary greatly depending on what kind of shop you are opening.

Marketing Tips

Since you'll need to raise a lot of money to operate a business like this, crowdfunding platforms like **www.GoFundMe.com** might be your best bet for cash and for public awareness. You should also reach out to businesses in the area that might be interested in working with you. Maybe there's a restaurant near the proposed location of your store, and the owners of that restaurant would be delighted if your customers came over for supper after indulging in an afternoon cup of tea.

54.   After School Program Worker

Business Overview

Do you want to be a teacher? Does spending your afternoons with kids sound exciting and fulfilling? Being an after school program worker could be the perfect job for you! After school program workers assist the leader of the after school program director in providing quality activities to children who stay at school for a few hours after classes end.

Education/Skills

You will need experience with childcare. Some combination of babysitting and volunteer work may be sufficient. If you're not yet qualified, think of creative ways that you can increase your child care experience. Some after school programs may require a bachelor's degree or associates degree, or at least some progress on one, but don't get discouraged — keep looking around.

Realistic Expectations

One of the best things about this job is that it shouldn't conflict with school hours — definitely a major benefit for teens! If you have childcare experience and good connections (maybe you participated in after school program when you were in elementary school, and you stayed in contact with the program director), you should be able to get a job.

Making Bank

The average salary of a childcare worker is $9.92 an hour.[52]

Business Equipment

Fortunately for you, no business equipment is required. All you might need is transportation to and from your place of work and a way to get into contact with the program director.

---

52. PayScale, 2017.

Marketing Tips

Get to know the after school program director at your school, if applicable. Ask around when you participate in childcare training, like first aid certification, and express your interest in after school programs.

55.   Professional Fundraiser

Business Overview

Many organizations either find themselves wanting to raise money for a special purpose or continually trying to raise more money for their projects and goals. If you have great people skills and don't mind driving all over town and knocking on doors, calling hundreds of phone numbers, or putting together packets of promotional material to mail out — and many other tasks — being a fundraiser could be great for you.

Education/Skills

Many people who work in fundraising as a long-term career have degrees in public administration. It's unlikely that a teen could get a salaried position at a nonprofit or company in their development or fundraising department. The good news is, however, that many teens participate in fundraisers on a grassroots level — hosting car washes for the cheerleaders, helping raise money for a local politician seeking office, and so forth.

Realistic Expectations

There are two problems with being a professional fundraiser as a teen. It will be hard to get non-volunteer work, and it will be hard to get steady work.

Making Bank

The average salary of a professional fundraiser is $22.43 an hour.[53]

Business Equipment

As long as you have a phone, reliable transportation, a computer, and a good Wi-Fi connection, you should be good to go. Fundraising might entail administering events with significant setup and teardown or mailing out promotional material, but the company or organization you're working for should generally supply the materials needed.

Marketing Tips

Getting in touch with all of the nonprofits and other organizations that might be in need of fundraising in your area would be a good first start. Maybe doing some volunteer fundraising work first — organizing a few successful events for your softball team, for instance — would be great experience and could eventually lead to work that pays.

56. Personal Concierge

Business Overview

When people think of doormen or concierges, they often think of middle-aged, polished gentlemen. But there's a demand for teenagers working as concierges. After all, the role of a concierge is to offer a welcome, establish a personal connection, and show the guest what he or she might be interested in about the hotel and local area. While the adult concierge is showing the teen's parents where the wine tasting is and encouraging them

---

53. PayScale, 2017.

to stop in the lounge, the teen concierge can, for instance, point out the water park nearby and explain that there are special activities and programs for teens at the hotel.

Education/Skills

Most concierge jobs require a high school diploma. More advanced, well-paying positions might require a hotel management degree. For a hotel to need or want teen concierges, it would probably be a resort town with lots of teen vacationers — not in a town where the local Hampton is mostly filled with businessmen going to meetings.

Realistic Expectations

If your area isn't geared toward teenage vacationers — you don't live near some pristine beach in Florida, for instance — you could always apply to be a regular concierge. If you're at least 16 years of age, you might be able to make the job work in either capacity. After all, hotels need workers at all hours, meaning that you could find hours to work that aren't during regular business hours — i.e., when you're generally in school.

Making Bank

The average salary of a concierge is $14.82 an hour.[54]

Business Equipment

You don't need any equipment for this one—not even your own computer. Transportation to the hotel would probably be a good idea since you might be working irregular hours.

---

54. PayScale, 2017.

Marketing Tips

Professionalism is key in this job — you are giving the first impression to the people who come to the hotel. Cultivating your own professional development will be key to marketing yourself as a good candidate to be a concierge. Be persistent — again, look into all of the hotels in your area — and demonstrate that you have the necessary skills.

57. Marketing Assistant

Business Overview

Marketing, quite simply, is the act of promoting an organization through any means. Advertising is perhaps the most commonly encountered form of marketing, although people who work in marketing do more than simply make advertisements.

A lot of companies want to market to teens. After all, teens are some of the most important users of today's top items — cell phones, social media, and so forth. If you're interested in the ways a company spreads its message and makes more money, a job in marketing could be right for you.

Education/Skills

Most marketing jobs require a college degree — often in marketing. At the very least, they require a high school diploma. But perhaps you could start as an intern at a local marketing firm in your town.

Realistic Expectations

Getting a job in marketing before you've gotten a high school diploma or even before you've gotten very far along in college will be difficult. Figure out why you like marketing and what experiences you have that would make you a qualified candidate. Marketing assistants work with data to analyze trends and preferences, and they have to be good at communicating to convey a company's message in the best-chosen language.

Making Bank

The average salary of a marketing assistant is $17.42 an hour.[55]

Business Equipment

You don't really need to own any equipment of your own, but will need to learn how to use software to make charts and more.

Marketing Tips

Have you helped advertise for events at your school? Are you doing well in your statistics class or English class? Make sure to build up experiences related to marketing — this will help you a lot when you try to get a job.

58.   Teach Swimming Lessons

Business Overview

Starting your own swimming school is a smart move for any swimming expert looking to share their methods and make some cash.

As a swimming teacher, you will work with a class or one-on-one with private students and coach them how to swim. You can hold these lessons at

---

55. PayScale, 2017.

your pool, at your students' pools, or at a rented location like a hotel or community center.

Education/Skills

Although any strong and confident swimmer can teach students how to swim, you may find it beneficial to have a CPR, first-aid, and swim instruction certification. These types of credentials will not only put you and your clients at ease, but they can also improve your lessons and make your business more attractive and official.

Realistic Expectations

Most swimming instructors' clients are parents who want their kids to learn how to swim. With the right advertising, this can be an easy market to tap into. Swimming lessons usually last from 30 minutes to an hour, depending on how many students you are working with, and you might teach the same student once a week for up to a year — giving you the chance to have steady work as well as free time.

Making Bank

The average salary of a lifeguard is $9.18 an hour.[56]

CASE STUDY: STACY CAPRIO

Stacy's Swim Lessons & Accelerated Growth Marketing
Plymouth, MN and Boston, MA
www.stacyswimlessons.weebly.com
www.acceleratedgrowthmarketing.com

When did you start your business?

I started the first one when I was 18. I started the second one when I was 21.

I was going to work at a country club as a lifeguard and swim instructor, but then I forgot to show up to my first two shifts in a row. So they fired me over email. This was before iPhone calendar reminders. At this point I realized I was lifeguard & WSI certified, had been swimming competitively for 14 years, had a pool in my backyard, and there was a real need for swimming lessons in my town, so I started a swimming lesson business. I started my SEM business after an SEM internship my junior year of college to get more experience working with startups in the Boston area and thought it would be fun to do. I actually got the idea for that business from my old swimming lesson business.

My swimming lesson business grew from $500 the first summer to over $4,000 in revenue and over 30 returning customers its third year. Some days were packed with 8-10 back to back lessons, which was exhausting but also fun because I got to play with kids in a pool. It was rewarding to see them get better and be genuinely grateful. I met some amazing families and people, some of whom I still stay in touch with to this day. My marketing business is also profitable but less packed, as I also currently have a full-time job.

---

56. PayScale, 2017.

Three satisfying moments: 1) On one of my 8 lesson days, in the middle of my last summer teaching swimming lessons, I was reflecting on how far my business had come. I realized how crazy it was that I was teaching full days of lessons and making more than I would have at any regular job while working the same hours without leaving my house; 2) Whenever kids or families would be genuinely appreciative, say thank you, and especially give me a handmade thank you card, I would get a feeling of satisfaction that could not have been bought with money; and 3) Sometimes a parent would ask me, "We found you on the first page of Google, how did you get there?" and I would smile happily.

People will tell you it won't be successful. They will smile and nod, but you will be able to tell they don't think it will work. Smile back and just do it. This is one of the times in life to listen to your gut feeling instead of what people are telling you. They are not trying to make you feel bad; they are just afraid of the unknown because starting a business defies all the social norms that are ingrained in them and they have never done something like it. My #1 piece of advice is only take advice from someone who has been where you want to be or who you would want to trade places with.

Business Equipment

Other than a pool, the most common equipment used by swimming instructors includes life jackets, kickboards, goggles, and floats.

Marketing Tips

Put up posters at community pools and other places where potential clients might see them. Distribute fliers, put ads in your community newspaper, ask for referrals from friends and family members, announce your services on social media, and create a swimming instructor website that stresses your location so parents can easily find you when they go to search online. You can even hand out business cards to parents at pools and beaches when you spot inexperienced swimmers.

Additional Resources

www.swimswam.com

www.swimmingtrainingcenter.com

www.swimlessonsuniversity.com

59.   Activist

Business Overview

Essentially, being an activist entails doing anything and everything that you can think of to further your cause. You'll meet with local leaders, spread awareness on a grassroots level, go to and host events related to your cause, organize protests, and more.

Education/Skills

You need to be an energetic and dedicated person, and you need to care deeply about your cause. Often, people become activists due to personal experiences or the experiences of those close to him or her. Losing a sibling to cancer could turn a person into an activist to find a cure for cancer, for instance. But just the experience isn't enough — you need to be able to communicate powerfully about the issue. You will have to convince others to care, too.

Realistic Expectations

People are sometimes apathetic about the things that matter most — including the things that matter most to you. So, sometimes it can be hard to get people to care and to invest time and money into your cause. Doing something to make a difference isn't that hard — organizing one 5k to raise money for children in poverty — but making a consistent, even daily effort to spread the news and think creatively about how to do so can be difficult and draining.

Making Bank

The amount of money that you will make may vary widely. You'll probably make nothing for yourself at first, but you can count it as a success from the outset if you're raising awareness and money for your cause.

Business Equipment

You might need many different types of equipment to spread your message. A computer and good Wi-Fi are a must, but your other needs could include graphic design software to create items; physical merchandise like t-shirts, mugs, and posters; tablecloths, plates, and more for events (you might rent them instead of buy them); and more.

Marketing Tips

If you don't just want your advocacy to be a side project but rather what you do for a living, you could ask some people to support you individually to make that a possibility. In other words, ask for contributions for yourself from a trusted group of supporters in addition to trying to raise money to support the cause.

60.   Spa Parties Consultant

Business Overview

A spa party consultant provides parties at spas. Basically, you will start your own business and begin advertising your services. You can offer specific spa party packages and provide some of the following services at your parties:

- Body Wrap

- Buff-n-Bronze Skin-Friendly Tanning

- Custom European Facial

- Gentleman's Facial

- Hot Stone Massage

- Massage

- Paraffin Foot and Hand Treatments

- Pedicure

- Reiki

- Teen Facial

- Zen Salt Glow

- Spa Facial

- Sugar Body Polish

- Toe Glow

- Yoga

You could also provide different packages, such as a birthday package or a mother and daughter package. Be creative and think of fun ideas.

Education/Skills

You do not need a degree, but you should be able to execute the various aspects of a spa party well. In other words, if you love to make facemasks, but it takes you a very long time to mix up the ingredients, you need to work on that before starting your business.

Realistic Expectations

It may be hard to get customers without having experience working in a spa or training as a massage therapist or esthetician. Nevertheless, a lot of women and girls like to have relaxing parties, so you would be marketing to a real and reliable interest. If you are professional, organized, and detail-oriented, your age and lack of formal experience probably won't matter that much — especially if you are persistent.

Making Bank

The average salary of a spa party consultant is $8.36 an hour.[57]

Business Equipment

You will need a variety of supplies, such as nail polish remover, cotton balls, nail files, orange sticks, nail polishes, scissors, mirrors, bowls, massage oils, wax products, towels, robes, and so on.

Marketing Tips

Provide a party for a neighbor. Invite all their friends and their parents and provide the party free of charge. You can also put together a free spa party for people in the community who deserve a day off, such as volunteers, veterans, servicemen and women, teachers, firefighters, police officers, and nonprofit administrators. Additionally, you can put together business parties and offer business owners a way to thank their employees. Invite them to have a relaxation day once a month or for special occasions throughout the year.

61.   Campaign Manager

Business Overview

As a campaign manager, you'll raise money, meet people, do some hiring and firing, perform communications-related work, and many other tasks, whether for a politician, a museum, or a company.

---

57. Glassdoor, 2017.

Education/Skills

You can get involved in political campaigns — handing out signs, making phone calls, knocking on doors, and more — from a very young age. You may have more experience than you think already. And if not, now is the time to start. But rest assured that this job isn't about a specific degree — it's all about connections.

Realistic Expectations

Campaign managers of any type work hard. Very hard. You need to devote a lot of time and effort to this job. Getting a campaign manager job as a teen will be difficult, but actually doing the job will be really hard, too. So don't be discouraged!

Making Bank

The average salary of a campaign manager is $25.93 an hour.[58]

Business Equipment

Social media skills and professional use of email are both musts. While you probably won't need to provide many materials, you'll need to know how to use a wide variety of equipment. Your job is to do whatever the candidate or campaign needs and coordinate everything the candidate or campaign does. Operating sound systems, setting up tables, speaking in public —you need to be ready to do it all.

---

58. PayScale, 2017.

Marketing Tips

Do as much volunteering as you can! Is there a school levy coming up where you live that you oppose? Is your state about to vote a social issue, and you have a strong opinion on the topic? Start doing something! Be creative and get involved in all the ways that you can.

62.   Elder Supervisor

Business Overview

Sometimes all senior citizens need to live on their own is someone to help perform a few daily tasks. As an elder supervisor, you will drive clients to appointments, run errands for them, and help with other day-to-day chores that they can't do themselves. This can be a very rewarding business. Not only can you earn decent money, but you will be making someone's life easier and helping them retain their independence.

Education/Skills

Since you will be providing non-medical services like errand-running and other chores around the house, most people don't need formal training for elder care. All you need is patience, a friendly personality, good communication skills, and a driver's license if you plan to run errands.

Realistic Expectations

Today, the American senior population is made up of around 41 million people, and that number is expected to double in just a couple of decades. Because new opportunities in senior care are created every day, this can be an easy market to tap into.

Making Bank

The average salary of an elder supervisor is $23.09 an hour.[59]

Business Equipment

Other than a vehicle, everything you need will probably be found at your clients' homes. Ask your clients if you should bring any equipment during your visits.

Marketing Tips

Even without extensive advertising, you probably have plenty of family and friends who either need help or know someone who does. Tell anyone you know that you're building your own business and are looking to gain experience by helping elders with day-to-day tasks. You can also hand out business cards, put up posters in community centers, libraries, hospitals, retirement homes, and other places where people will see them. To get even more attention, create a blog or website, take out classified newspaper ads, ask for referrals from friends and family members, and announce your service on social media.

Additional Resources

www.aging-parents-and-elder-care.com

www.seniorerrandservice.com

http://seniorservicebusiness.com

---

59. PayScale, 2017.

63.   Consultant

Business Overview

As a consultant, you'll work with clients, conducting research, learning about their business, and making recommendations.

Education/Skills

Most consultants are college graduates and often work for consulting firms. The best option for you would be to start your own consulting group.

Realistic Expectations

If you are able to market yourself as an expert—and have a wide potential network of clients—you have a good chance of breaking into the field.

Making Bank

The average salary of a business consultant is $34.26 an hour.[60]

Business Equipment

Generally, consulting involves you going to the business —not the other way around—so you won't need a lot of equipment.

Marketing Tips

Most teen consultants help adults determine effective marketing strategies to reach teens. You could create some good opportunities for yourself by being a teen trying to figure out how to market to teens.

---

60. PayScale, 2017.

64.   Manicurist

Business Overview

Have you ever painted your own fingernails? When you do, do you get more polish on the rest of you than you get on your nails? If your answers were "yes" and "no" (in that order), being a manicurist could be the perfect job for you.

Education/Skills

You will need to get a license from your state's Board of Barbering and Cosmetology, which may require periodic renewal, for a fee. Before you can take the test, you have to complete courses at a licensed Cosmetology school, and/or apprentice for a certain number of hours. Part of your schooling will teach you about your state's sanitation laws, which are *very* important to the health of your clients and the success of your business. Good communication skills, attention to detail, and a little artistic ability will be helpful.

Realistic Expectations

You need to keep very good track of income vs. expense, and you will spend much of your off-hours building your business in ways other than actively doing manicures. Look around your chosen location at similar businesses and decide what you can feasibly charge (and what you need to charge to cover costs). The best part about being your own boss is that you can decide what services you want to offer. The range of services you provide are entirely up to you.

Making Bank

The average salary of a manicurist is $11.33 an hour.[61]

Business Equipment

You will need a professional set of tools, cleaning supplies, possibly a pedicure tub and chair, a manicure table and chairs, and oodles of nail polish. State law will require you to keep certain chemicals on hand to sanitize your tools and equipment. If you offer nail art you should keep small paintbrushes, acrylic paint, gemstones, and foil tape on hand. There are several specialty services that manicurists can offer, and all of them require specialized inventory. Artificial nail services, gel polish systems, paraffin wax services, hot stone pedicures — the list can go on and on.

Marketing Tips

Take advantage of the tools you probably already have on your phone. Instagram, Facebook, and Twitter are all great tools to advertise your business to potential clients, but you've got to keep up with them! Create business accounts that only feature photos of your own work, and make sure you post regularly. Also, use your friends and family as guinea pigs for practice and for your portfolio. Leave stacks of business cards wherever you're allowed and network with other professionals in the beauty industry.

Additional Resources

www.beautyschoolsdirectory.com/faq/state_req.php www.payscale .com/research/US/Job=Manicurist_or_Pedicurist/Hourly_Rate

---

61. PayScale, 2017.

65. Hairstylist

Business Overview

If you like to make people feel good about themselves, perhaps becoming a hairstylist is the right career path for you.

Education/Skills

You will need to get a license from your state's Board of Barbering and Cosmetology. You have to complete courses at a licensed cosmetology school, and/or apprentice for a certain number of hours. Often, hair is part of a bigger program called cosmetology, which also includes nails, some skin care, and waxing services. You will learn about your state's sanitation laws, which are *very* important to the health of your clients and the success of your business. If you want to color hair as well as cut it, an eye for color and some understanding of the chemistry of the process will help. Good communication skills are a must.

Realistic Expectations

You'll get some experience while you're at school, since many schools offer deeply discounted services to people in the community, and you should make use of your friends and family, to build your skill set and your portfolio of work. Take as many "Before & After" photos of your work as you can to make people feel comfortable with your skill level. You can work on your own in a rented space, as a traveling stylist, or you can rent space from an existing salon.

Making Bank

The average salary of a hairstylist is $9.72 an hour.[62]

Business Equipment

You will need an adjustable chair (for your own benefit), a mirror, a sink, and some rather expensive tools, which you'll probably acquire while still in school. Again, your state will require you to comply with sanitation laws by using certain chemical-cleaning agents. You'll also need many different types of combs and brushes and lots of styling tools and hair products. If you offer hair-coloring services, you'll need a large color inventory. If you offer special occasion styling, you'll need a supply of bobby pins, elastics, and other hair-fastening devices.

---

62. PayScale, 2017.

Marketing Tips

Advertise your business to potential clients using Instagram, Facebook, and Twitter, and be sure to post regularly. Only post photos of your own work, and use your friends, family, and cosmetology schoolmates whenever you can.

Additional Resources

www.money.usnews.com/careers/best-jobs/hairdresser

www.beautyschoolsdirectory.com/faq/state_req.php

66.   Trivia Night Host

Business Overview

You'll essentially be the emcee at restaurants, fundraisers, birthday parties, and more, facilitating as people play trivia games. You'll announce the topics of the questions, read out the individual questions, and tell people when their answers are right or wrong.

Education/Skills

You don't need any formal education, but it would be helpful if you're interested in everything from science to history. Writing skills—knowing how to make the questions clear and interesting—will also be important. So if you're a science and history buff who does well in your English classes—and you have some public speaking experience, you will be good to go!

Realistic Expectations

A lot of the places where trivia nights are held may not be accessible to you since a common place for trivia nights is bars. Some restaurant or coffee shop owners may not trust that a teen has what it takes to keep an audience engaged and entertained. But if you can find some relatively steady gigs, you could have a fun and profitable job.

Making Bank

You could charge a set amount for a night or an afternoon—$100, for instance.

Business Equipment

You may need to design visual aids or cards for the trivia questions. And you will need to have some sort of transportation to the places where you'll be hosting game nights.

Marketing Tips

You should call many of the restaurants in your area—as well as the non-profit organizations—and ask if they are willing to try you out as a trivia game host. A restaurant or organization is not going to want to spend money on your service if you don't bring in more customers for them.

67. Personal Trainer

Business Overview

Personal trainers work with clients one-on-one in a gym setting to help them meet their exercise and fitness goals.

Education/Skills

Many certifications require that you are more than 16 years of age. If you have some kind of certification and a lot of experience in sports and exercise, and are willing to invest your spare time into reading and learning more about fitness techniques and safety precautions, you could acquire the necessary skills.

Realistic Expectations

It is easy to get certified, although it may cost some money to do so. Do you want to work with fellow teens, adults, or the elderly? Figuring out how to get clients and where to meet them might be difficult. You'll have to exercise an entrepreneurial spirit.

Making Bank

The average salary of a personal trainer is $20.17 an hour.[63]

Business Equipment

If your family has a home gym, you'll have a leg up on logistics and transportation costs—your clients can come to you! If not, you'll have to con-

---

63. PayScale, 2017.

tact local gyms and may even have to pay for your own membership as well.

Marketing Tips

Your clients will probably start out as friends or friends of friends — people who know you well enough to know that you will do a good job. Make your friends and family aware of your new business, and if you're well connected with sports and exercise groups in your area, you should be able to get clients.

Chapter 7

#hashtags and the Internet: Options for the Digitally Savvy

68. Social Media Influencer

Business Overview

Teens today have had more early exposure to computers, the internet, and smartphones than any other generation in history. Many teens know how to use social media with greater dexterity than adults. Why not use those web skills to make money?

Using Instagram, Twitter, Facebook, YouTube, and Snapchat, you'll want to attract a following and get people to listen to what you post. You may even be hired by a business to help with its social media use.

Education/Skills

You don't need an advanced degree to make this business idea work—all you need is a lot of social media savvy and enough luck to make you go viral.

Realistic Expectations

Most people won't make it big with their YouTube channels or Instagram feeds, so you need to try your best and keep your expectations low. Even if a lot of people enjoy watching your videos or looking at your photos, there's still quite a jump from that to making money. Do lots of research into social media trends—read blogs, keep up on what's trending on Facebook, etc.—and be aware of what your intended market is,

Making Bank

The average salary of a social media influencer is $19.71 an hour.[64]

Business Equipment

A good camera, computer, video equipment, and Wi-Fi are all potential necessities for this job.

Marketing Tips

Show potential sponsors that you know how to market to teens. Plenty of companies are willing to pay social media influencers to market their products to their followers. The idea is that potential customers trust people like you more than generic ads. If you want to blog, the best way to start getting attention is to post three times a week—although make sure you actually have something interesting to say. If you want to make your mark via Snapchat or Instagram, make sure to invest in some very good photo editing software—and learn how to use it. If you're on Twitter or Facebook, remember that the highest number of followers is not necessarily better—you just need to make sure that your intended market is seeing your posts.

---

64. PayScale, 2017.

In all areas of social media, you'll need to have consistent branding—it should be clear to your viewers what you're all about, whether it's lifestyle advice or political commentary.

Additional Resources

www.mashable.com/2016/08/16/25-tips-becoming-online-influencer /#I5Y2Yt9mwqqt

www.brandwatch.com/2015/08/asktheexperts-17-rules-to-follow-for -becoming-an-influencer

69. Technology Consultant/Helper

Business Overview

You will be instructing people on how to use technology and fixing people's printers, computers, phones, etc. when those gadgets aren't working properly. You will need to be knowledgeable on the basics of how electronics work, as well as clever at deciphering a how-to manual and finding the problem via physical examination of the device. Your goal should be to make your clients' technological devices work as quickly and as best as they can—and if repairs do need to be made, you want to find the cheapest solution.

Education/Skills

You don't need any kind of degree to establish your credibility with computers, but you do need to have a lot of experience.

Realistic Expectations

Your best chance of breaking into this industry is by cultivating a network of people who can recommend your services to others—word-of-mouth advertising—and creating a well-designed, appealing website that will attract people to your business.

Making Bank

The average salary of a technical consultant is $35.54 an hour.[65]

CASE STUDY:
NICK ANTONELLE

Honor Roll Technology
Long Valley, NJ
www.honorrolltechnology.com

I started Honor Roll Technology in late 2015. I was 12 years old at the time.

What I like most about my business is that I get to make the rules. Unlike school, where I have an assignment due on a Tuesday, as example, I can determine when I get my work done and my deadline. It makes me feel good to have some authority like that. I also really like to see the smile on my clients' faces when I'm able to help them with their issues. I like that it gives me the opportunity to handle other aspects not necessarily related to technology, like dealing with people, negotiating rates, customer service and marketing through social media.

My best moment as a teen business owner was when I received word that I got my first client ever in the business world. I listened to a voicemail message from a family friend that she wanted to hire me. I had the biggest smile and realized that I COULD help people who aren't as experienced with technology. Getting that call told me that I could be successful as a business owner. I called my friend Braden who helps me soon after that call

65. PayScale, 2017.

and said "We got our first project!" He was shocked, but also very excited. That is my best moment in the business world so far. I experience that same feeling every time I get a new client!

The advice I have for a teen who would like to start a business is to do what you love and do what is fun for you. Don't do something you wouldn't like doing because the passion for starting that type of business won't last. Do something you'll have fun doing and will enjoy working on. I started Honor Roll Technology since I like technology and computers. For me, it's really not work!

Business Equipment

You'll certainly need a computer for answering correspondence and keeping up your website, and you'll probably need some software—maybe some graphic design software—to make your website look nice. If you have a car, you'll be able to go to customers' houses and check on items that may be difficult to transport like TVs or big printers.

Marketing Tips

On your website, you should list what services you offer specifically, give a clear idea about how much your services cost, and make the method of contacting you easy. So that your help can extend to people outside the city or town where you live, you could potentially offer some services over Skype, especially if the focus is more on trying to teach the person how to use a certain aspect of technology.

70.   App Creator

Business Overview

There's no set way or path to becoming an app creator because you can create an app for just about anything—and who knows how you will get the idea for your idea. But the steps to design it and market it will look similar for everyone.

Education/Skills

No education is needed to create an app—but some skills are. You'll need to have basic coding skills if you want to design the app features yourself.

Realistic Expectations

Because it's relatively easy to make an app, you'll have tough competition. And you may even get a lot of people to use your app without making any money off of it. Nevertheless, if you're a creative person with good design skills who has a lot of clever ideas, you can keep making apps until something takes off!

Making Bank

The average salary of an app creator is $32.60 an hour.[66]

Business Equipment

Good software is needed, but not much else.

Marketing Tips

You need to make sure there's a market for your app; thoroughly investigate which apps are trending and why. Often, apps that improve something or make life easier in some way tend to succeed. You also might be hired to make an app for an organization, such as an app for a local business. Have a clear idea of what you want to do. Once you publish your Android or iPhone app, you'll have to decide whether it should cost money or be free. Having the app cost money obviously increases your chances of making a profit, but people are *way* more likely to use free apps.

Additional Resources

www.blog.udemy.com/making-an-app/

---

66. PayScale, 2017.

71. Virtual Assistant

Business Overview

Today, businesses are starting to see the benefits of hiring remote employees. They are hard and competitive workers, they are available at all times of the day, they cut hours from the employer's workweek, and they save the business money by not needing an onsite office.

As a virtual assistant, you will work from home to provide the services that many small businesses and entrepreneurs need. These services will differ from job-to-job but may include things like web design, bookkeeping, marketing, customer service, writing press releases, managing social media accounts, research, graphic design, transcription, video editing, and composing and answering email.

Education/Skills

You can become a virtual assistant no matter what kind of education, skills, or experience you have. A good virtual assistant will also be organized, professional, resourceful, and good at managing their time without much supervision.

Realistic Expectations

The number of successful virtual assistants is growing every day. This means that there is a lot of competition out there, but it also means that business owners are becoming more open to having remote employees on their team, which gives you the opportunity to find first-time clients and build your reputation as an excellent virtual assistant.

Making Bank

The average salary of a virtual assistant is $15.61 an hour.[67]

Business Equipment

Some of the essentials in a virtual assistant's armory include a computer, telephone, internet connection, and office supplies.

Marketing Tips

Most clients who need a virtual assistant will be doing their shopping online, so that's where you should go to land your first gig. Create a website that features background info, reviews, and the types of services you offer. Another good way to drum up attention is to post on social media about your business, start a blog, and network with other virtual assistants. You can also find first-time clients on sites like **www.freelancer.com, www.taskrabbit.com,** and **www.upwork.com.**

Additional Resources

www.thevahandbook.com

www.vanetworking.com

72. Smartphone Repair

Business Overview

Smartphones are not only more popular than ever, but they are necessary in our increasingly digital lives. If you have a special knack for repairing

---

67. PayScale, 2017.

and troubleshooting smartphones, you can easily turn that knowledge into a profitable business.

Education/Skills

There are no formal educational requirements for this business. All you really need is a steady hand and experience repairing smartphones quickly and efficiently.

Realistic Expectations

Smartphone repair services are easy to start. And since almost everyone has a smartphone nowadays, there are plenty of clients. If you have the skills to fix these phones and advertise your services, business won't be too hard to find.

Needless to say, it can be tough to make a living in smartphone repair depending on your location; but like most home-based businesses, you will have very little overhead and will be able to charge less than your competitors — making it easier to find first-time clients and build your reputation.

Making Bank

The average salary of a smartphone repair person is $10.80 an hour.[68]

Business Equipment

There are a lot of tools needed to run a successful smartphone repair business. Some of the most common items include a universal smartphone tool

---

68. PayScale, 2017.

kit, anti-static brushes, a digitizer separator machine, isopropyl alcohol, a heat gun, and tweezers.

Marketing Tips

Even without extensive advertising, you probably have a few friends and family members who either need help with their smartphone or know someone who does.

You can also create blogs, websites, and social media pages, hand out business cards, put up posters, write smartphone-related articles for newspapers and webzines, take out classified newspaper ads, ask for referrals from people you know, and announce your service on social media.

Additional Resources

www.cellphonerepair.com

www.ifixit.com

73. Computer Repair Specialist

Business Overview

Computer repair specialists are needed everywhere. And whether you can crack open a system unit and have it running like new or you're simply familiar with the basics like removing viruses and installing software, you can find someone who is willing to pay for your help.

A computer repair specialist should be able to provide most of the following services:

- Troubleshooting small errors

- Removing and installing new hard drives

- Installing additional memory

- Virus removal

- Data recovery, full system recovery, and backup of data

- Diagnosing network and modem problems

- Installing additional hard drives, zip drives, or DVD/CD readers/writers

- Installing software

- Cleaning the computer system

Education/Skills

Although there are computer courses and certifications that would be beneficial, there are no formal educational requirements for this business. All you really need is experience with computer hardware and the knowledge of how to repair it. Good customer service skills are also a big plus; and if you intend to offer onsite repairs, you will need a driver's license and access to a car.

Realistic Expectations

Computer repair services are easy to start. And since almost everyone has a computer nowadays, there are more clients out there than ever before.

This is a tough business to make a living in, but like most home-based businesses, you will have very little overhead and will be able to charge less than your competitors—making it easier to find first-time clients.

Making Bank

The average salary of a computer repair specialist is $13.76 an hour.[69]

Business Equipment

To run a successful computer repair business, you will need repair and diagnostic equipment and software, spare hard drives, RAM, cases, and cables. You will also need basic tools like pliers, cutters, screwdrivers, nut drivers, straps, zip ties, flashlights, and electronic cleaning materials.

Marketing Tips

Even without extensive advertising, you probably have plenty of friends and family members who either need help with their computer or know someone who does. Tell anyone you know that you're building your computer repair business and are looking for clients and experience. You can also create blogs, websites, and social media pages, hand out business cards, put up posters, write computer-related articles for newspapers and webzines, take out classified newspaper ads, ask for referrals from people you know, and announce your service on social media.

Additional Resources

www.technibble.com

www.thetechmentor.com

---

69. PayScale, 2017.

74.   Videographer

Business Overview

Do you enjoy using a video camera to capture moments as they happen? Do you know how to use angles, lighting, pacing, zooms, pans, and cuts to create a smooth and interesting video? Perhaps being behind that camera can make you some money.

As a professional videographer, you can video weddings, childbirths, birthday parties, anniversaries, reunions, and a variety of other special events. Other duties may include video editing, adding special effects or music, transferring videos to DVDs, or uploading videos to the internet. Along with recording special events, videographers can also find work shooting documentaries, commercials, and films.

Education/Skills

There's a difference between simply pointing a camera and being a videographer. If you want to survive in this business, you need creativity, organization, patience, interpersonal skills, a good eye for detail, and the technical ability to work your camera and video-editing software. There are college majors dedicated to filmmaking, but you can easily develop your skills more economically through online tutorials, local classes and workshops, and practice.

Realistic Expectations

All sorts of people need videographers. There's plenty of talented competition in the industry, but with the right skills and equipment, you can easily break into the market through family, friends, pro bono work, and a little advertising.

Making Bank

The average salary of a videographer is $20.71 an hour.[70]

---

70. PayScale, 2017.

CASE STUDY: TIM MALY

I started my business a week after I turned 16.

I think the thing I like the most about running my own business is definitely being able to work on my own time, and to work at home if I want to — also the ability to work in coffee shops, which can lead to some interesting conversations and opportunities at the least expected time.

There have been quite a lot of satisfying moments, but I love covering events the first time they're put on. I never know if they'll still be around the next year, but if they are, it's always way bigger. Knowing that I shot it back when it hadn't been done before and when they had no budget is always extremely satisfying.

For advice, I've found muuuuch much more help in the quest of self-awareness than anything else — basically just Gary Vaynerchuk line of thinking. Have self-awareness, patience, and always offer more in an interaction, which could be as simple as just brightening up a customer's day with some good vibes!

Tim Maly, who currently lives in Fargo, North Dakota, has always been a filmmaker, although every one that he talked to would ask him what he actually wanted to be, as if filmmaking wasn't a possibility. But then he dropped out of high school at the age of 16 to pursue his dream. It's been about a year since he started his business, and he has shot hundreds of videos and has absorbed a massive amount of information about everything from ROI to human nature and his own inner workings.

Business Equipment

As a professional videographer, you will need a lot of gear. Some of the basics include a video camera, lenses, lighting equipment, a tripod, boom pole, shotgun microphone, shock mount, a powerful computer with video-editing software, and tapes, memory cards, or DVDs to store your footage. You might also need a car.

Marketing Tips

When you're first starting out in the video industry, it's important to have examples of your work to show potential clients. These can be local concerts, short films, weddings—anything that shows what you and your camera are capable of. If you want even more experience in the industry before setting out on your own, contact video production companies or hotel audio visual departments and work your way through lower-level jobs, internships, and apprenticeships.

Once you have a portfolio showcasing your talent and experience, you can start hunting for gigs. Hand out business cards, put up posters, take out classified newspaper ads, and ask for referrals from past clients and other people you know. You should also build a strong internet presence through social media, personal blogs and websites, and video hosting sites like YouTube and Vimeo.

Additional Resources

www.videomaker.com

http://nofilmschool.com

www.creativelive.com

75.   Bookkeeper

Business Overview

Do you like keeping track of things and working with numbers? Then bookkeeping is the perfect job for you. There are many small businesses that need a smart employee to do basic bookkeeping — something you can pick up quickly, if you haven't already.

Your basic duties will be to keep records of the business's earnings, losses, and payables. You'll be dealing with invoices, receipts, and spreadsheets. Other duties might include:

- Payroll

- Billing

- Financial statements

- Bank transactions

Education/Skills

Bookkeeping is easier to get into than regular accounting services, and most employers do not ask for a CPA or any other accounting degree. Knowledge of basic accounting will be helpful in this field. You should also have a basic understanding of spreadsheets and accounting software.

Realistic Expectations

Steadiness and discretion will go a long way toward a business being willing to trust you with important confidential documents. The business will have to believe that you are reliable, so any past experience will help.

Making Bank

The average salary of a bookkeeper is $16.42 an hour.[71]

Business Equipment

You should invest in good accounting software and also have a variety of ledgers on hand. When you keep books you want to be sure to log the information in the computer and in the ledger, to have both available to the client.

Marketing Tips

Contact small businesses in your area to see if they are in need of a bookkeeper, place ads in the local paper, and become involved in your local chamber of commerce.

Additional Resources

www.entrepreneur.com/article/77962

76.   Tax Services

Business Overview

To many people, the U.S. tax code is nothing but a whirlwind of ever-changing terminology about deductions, credits, tax rates, and numbers. So, to avoid all the confusion and anxiety and maximize their deductions, these folks are eager to pay someone else to deal with it.

---

71. PayScale, 2017.

With a tax preparation business, you will work with these clients and businesses to help prepare their tax returns throughout the year.

Education/Skills

Contrary to what most people think, you don't need to be a certified public accountant or even a college graduate to work as a tax professional. If you are good with numbers and work well with people, you have what it takes.

If you need to brush up on how the tax code works, you can get all the tax training and preparation courses you need from local tax service companies or community colleges. And be sure to check with your city or state to see if they have any licensing requirements for professional tax preparers.

Realistic Expectations

More people are turning to independent tax preparers than ever before. Competition is out there, but if you have the skills to run and advertise a basic tax service, clients shouldn't be too hard to find. You will have very little overhead and will be able to charge less than your competitors.

Making Bank

The average pay of a tax preparer is $12.20 an hour.[72]

Business Equipment

At the very least, most tax preparers will need a computer, a printer and scanner, Wi-Fi, office supplies, tax preparation software, and possibly a

---

72. PayScale, 2017.

Preparer Taxpayer Identification Number (PTIN) and Electronic Filers Identification Number (EFIN) from the IRS.

Marketing Tips

When tax seasons roll around, tell anyone you know that you're building your business and are looking for clients. You can also hand out business cards, put up posters, create a blog or website, write tax-related articles for newspapers and webzines, take out classified newspaper ads, ask for referrals from people you know, and announce your service on social media.

Additional Resources

www.taxingsubjects.com

www.theincometaxschool.com

77.　YouTuber

Business Overview

Like most people, you've probably wandered over to YouTube for all sorts of things—entertainment, advice, news, cat videos. The essentials. But did you know that a lot of the videos you watch are actually making money for the video creators?

If you can make interesting videos, you might be able make some money too. As a professional YouTuber, you will have endless options to choose from. All you have to do is create valuable content and get it out there.

Education/Skills

Surprise! Other than knowing a few computer basics, there's no formal education or skills required to be a professional YouTuber. Any education or skills you have can be useful depending on the type of content you make. And people with video editing experience will have an advantage.

Realistic Expectations

Unfortunately, it's not the easiest thing to get noticed as a new YouTuber. Not only does it take a lot of unpaid time and effort to create quality content, but there's also a lot of competition out there. Approximately 300 hours of content is uploaded to YouTube every minute, and it's easy to get lost in the crowd.

Fortunately, there's over a billion people who visit YouTube on a regular basis. So, if you know your audience and can create content that appeals to them, it's possible to build a YouTube channel that will attract viewers and potentially become a source of revenue. When creating your channel, the best way to succeed is to find a niche that is unexploited and dominate it.

Making Bank

When you are making money, it's probably going to be coming from the ads you allow on your video's page.

Because the money you make through YouTube ads depends on how many viewers click or view the ads, the size of your audience is a big factor in determining how much you earn. On average, a YouTuber can expect to make around $1 to $4 for every 1,000 views. YouTubers can make even more money if they put affiliate links in their descriptions, sell merchandise related to their channel (like music, shirts, hats, toys, pictures, original artwork, and DVDs).[73]

Business Equipment

Your business equipment will vary depending on what kind of videos you make. At the very least, you will need Wi-Fi, a video camera, a computer, and possibly video-editing software.

Marketing Tips

YouTube may be a video-hosting platform, but it's also a social media service like Facebook and Twitter. To get views and build a loyal following, you not only have to create great content, but you have to engage with the world, connect with viewers and similar creators, and spread the word about your channel without being aggressive or annoying.

It's also a good idea to develop a strong internet presence on sites other than YouTube. You can do this through Facebook, Twitter, Snapchat, internet forums, personal blogs and websites, and any place where your audience might visit. And the best thing about YouTube is that if viewers like your content, they will spread the word for you.

Additional Resources

www.google.com/adsense/start

www.patreon.com

www.channelpages.com

---

73. Chron, 2017.

78. Blogger

Business Overview

If you're tech-savvy and like writing, being a blogger is your dream come true. You can blog about virtually anything. You choose your hours, and the best part is that you get to ramble on about whatever it is you're passionate about.

Education/Skills

You don't need any special education for this position. Having a basic understanding of the internet will be helpful.

Realistic Expectations

You may not make much money blogging, but if you love doing it, it can be a side project. It's best to start out with no eye on the prize—simply do what you love and read up on how you can monetize it to make some extra cash.

Making Bank

The majority of bloggers don't make enough money to support themselves full-time. That's just a fact. According to Lifehacker, this pie chart pretty closely represents what bloggers actually make every month.[74]

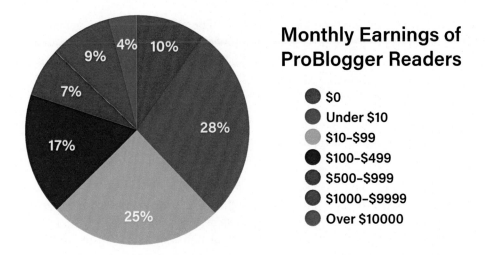

74. Pinola, 2014.

CASE STUDY:
GILLIAN LYN MAXWELL

LifeoftheAmbitious.com
Palm Beach, Florida and Tallahassee,
Florida
LifeoftheAmbitious.com

When did you start your business?

I started it in 2012 at 14-years-old.

When I started it, it was a personal endeavor. The site was an outlet I used to express my views on the fashion world for myself, to get away from the outside world. The idea came from viewing online bloggers with their amazing fashion experiences and outfits and being in awe.

I like waking up and working with the same people everyday. The best part is doing what I like to do and being in charge of how to grow a vision that I created, instead of being under someone else's creative direction. There is nothing like watching your staff members grow individually as a people and professionally through their work with your company.

The most satisfying moment I have had, was to see how my vision has had an affect on other individuals. This is the best feeling ever, especially when there is an emotional tie on top of the professional bonds I have created.

Go for your dreams. DO NOT take no for an answer. If you get stopped one way, you push through and create another. Understand that sacrifices will have to be made and that this type of lifestyle is not for everyone. Sometimes the dream of being an entrepreneur and the reality are two different things, and hard work comes before influence and following. Also, you CANNOT do it alone —ever. So, the people that are riding with your vision deserve respect and trust, but also watch those people and have a view on what to do next for each and every outcome and each and every position on your team. Growth takes time.

Business Equipment

All you need is a computer and a blog host. Common hosts include Word-press and Blogger, but there are tons to choose from. Do some research, and be sure to check out the additional resources to get a feel for your best option.

Marketing Tips

The best marketing strategy, first and foremost, is to choose a blog topic that is very specific and fills a niche. If you're all over the place, you won't attract the kinds of readers that will constantly engage.

There are tons of ways to market your blog, but the most important thing is to sync it with your other social media sites and to use very targeted keywords in your post titles.

Additional Resources

So You Want to Start a Blog: A Step-by-Step Guide to Starting a Fun & Profitable Blog by Rebekah Sack

www.bloggingtips.com

https://wordpress.com

79. E-Commerce/eBay Reseller

Business Overview

Do you ever think to yourself that you could resell items at a higher price? Then you might consider becoming an e-commerce reseller. The idea is to acquire products and then turn around and sell them for a profit. Aficionados of all stripes will likely find ways to acquire great items for resale.

E-commerce businesses have a couple of options to choose from. They can either build their own site to sell their products or use an already established marketplace like eBay, Etsy, and Amazon.

Education/Skills

There is no formal education required for this job. A technical or business background would be helpful. Also, check with your city or state to see what kinds of licenses you might need before you begin operation.

Realistic Expectations

There's good news and bad news. The good news is that people are spending more and more money online than ever before. Not only that, but e-commerce businesses are cheap and easy to start and can be run from home. The bad news is that it's not as easy to succeed in an e-commerce business as it is to start it. The competition is tough, and it takes a lot of time and work, but with creative ideas and a lot of dedication, you can do well for yourself.

Making Bank

The average salary of an ecommerce specialist is $22.60 an hour.[75]

Business Equipment

At the very least, you will need a computer and Wi-Fi. Depending on the business, some sellers may also need a web hosting service, shopping cart software, a credit card processor, a camera, space to store inventory, and shipping supplies.

Marketing Tips

Once you decide what you are selling and whom you are selling it to, choose a unique and memorable business name that your customers will remember. After registering your name, you can start securing websites, domain names, user names, blogs, and social media profiles.

To be successful in the e-commerce business, you will also need a strategy for getting customers to these websites and marketplace profiles. You can do this through email campaigns, social media ads, pay-per-click advertising, and search engine optimization (SEO).

Additional Resources

www.ecommerceguide.com

www.shopify.com

www.opencart.com

---

75. Glassdoor, 2016.

80.   Stock Photo Seller

Business Overview

To put it simply, stock photography is when you upload your pictures to an online photo library for clients to purchase. If they buy your photo, you earn commission. It's a great way for both professional and amateur photographers to make money off whatever high-quality photos they have lying around.

Education/Skills

There's no formal education needed for this job. Along with basic photography skills, you will need to be familiar with the stock photo world so that you have an eye for the types of pictures businesses are looking for.

Realistic Expectations

Stock photography earnings generally aren't more than supplementary. Still, if you have hundreds or even thousands of high-quality pictures uploaded to the top stock photo websites, earning hundreds of dollars a month is not impossible. And with time and experience, you may be able to turn it into a full-time business.

Making Bank

How much you earn per sale will depend on the quality of your photographs, the amount of sales you make, and which stock photo agency you work with. On a site like **www.dreamstime.com**, you can earn $5 for every purchase; while sites like **www.bigstockphoto.com**, **www.shutterstock. com**, and **www.istockphoto.com** can earn stock photographers between

$0.25 and $3 a sale. This may seem like small change, but if you have hundreds of popular photos, the money starts to add up.

Business Equipment

You will need a camera, a computer, photo editing software, and Wi-Fi.

Marketing Tips

The best part about stock photography is that the site you work with tends to do all the marketing for you. You simply upload your photo and wait for the royalties. For sites like ShutterStock, you are required to submit 10 pictures, and 7 of them have to be accepted. If your pictures don't cut it, you can't try again for another month.

When submitting stock photo applications, make sure your photos are clear and sharp and feature things that businesses are likely to buy. Once you're accepted, you can start uploading your stash.

Additional Resources

www.sellinggraphics.com/

www.slrphotographyguide.com

www.makeuseof.com/tag/places-sell-your-photos-online

81.　Device Creator

Business Overview

You'll essentially be an inventor of new technological devices, following in the footsteps of the people who invented the iPhone, the PC, and more.

Education/Skills

You don't need a degree to do this, but you do need a lot of ingenuity and creativity. You have to both imagine and execute—not only do you have to come up with a great idea, but also you have to figure out how to make it a reality. You'll need to document your idea at every step of the way and investigate thoroughly to make sure that no one has invented it already.

Realistic Expectations

Once you've made a prototype you're convinced that your device should be sold everywhere, the next step is to apply for a patent—which will cost a lot of money upfront, potentially several thousand dollars.

Making Bank

The amount of money that you could make is hard to estimate with any reliability. You could end up being several thousand dollars in the hole, but even in that scenario you will have gained valuable experience that will almost certainly help you in the future as you continue to think up new devices.

Business Equipment

The equipment will vary depending upon what you are trying to make, but you will definitely need a notebook or binder for documentation—

drawings of what you want it to look like in the early stages, records of your legal research, etc.

Marketing Tips

If you document every stage of the creation process, and do your research on the patent process, you are far more likely to be successful with your product.

Additional Resources

www.entrepreneur.com/article/77962

Chapter 8

For the Foodies

82. Caterer

Business Overview

Caterers provide the food for gatherings of all sizes. When you go to pot-luck parties, do you pride yourself on always having the most delicious dish, or the most adorable individual desserts? Do you have a passion for good food and want to share it with the world? Catering might be the perfect job for you.

Education/Skills

You will need to learn good food safety habits and rules, since local laws will apply to you as they do to any establishment that feeds the public. Math and organization skills will be important because you're feeding much larger groups who want their food ready and hot at the same time. Cooking skills go without saying, and meal planning of course. Learn from the good cooks in your family, and take classes through adult education programs in your area or through culinary stores whenever possible.

Realistic Expectations

Local regulations are a matter of public record and can be discovered easily. Potential customers will doubt your abilities based on your age. Start with small gatherings for friends and family and work your way up, getting references and testimonials whenever possible. You will be working nights and weekends, standing on your feet for hours in uncomfortably hot kitchens, and lifting large quantities of food. Many caterers are responsible for the setup and breakdown of banquet or buffet tables and equipment, so if you can, get a group of friends to help you.

Making Bank

The average salary of a caterer is $11.95 an hour.[76]

Business Equipment

You need basically everything that you would find in a standard kitchen, from appliances to plastic wrap. You can hopefully use your home kitchen most of the time, though you may need an extra refrigerator specifically for event food. You are also going to need decorative dishes and platters, chafing dishes and fuel, and a means of transportation — for you and the food!

Marketing Tips

Word-of-mouth is the best kind of advertising, since people who've eaten your delicious food will know just what their friends are missing. Partner with event venues, florists, DJs, party stores, and anybody else you can think of that could play a part in a large get-together.

---

76. PayScale, 2017.

Additional Resources

www.wikihow.com/Start-a-Catering-Business

**www.smallbusiness.chron.com/start-catering-business-home-260
.html www.payscale.com/research/US/Job=Caterer/Hourly_Rate**

83. Personal Chef

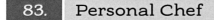

Business Overview

Being a personal chef can be a much more intimate experience than catering for big events. Most personal chefs work for people who are simply too
busy to cook for themselves. It may be a single person with a demanding
job, or a couple who travel a lot for work, or maybe you'll specialize in
family dinners to help busy parents. Whatever business model you choose,
if you're dedicated and responsible, you can be successful in this career.

Education/Skills

You will need good food safety habits, though nothing as strict as what restaurants must comply with. Nutritional knowledge is a great thing to have, and many clients may be hiring you to help them eat healthier. Organization and meal planning skills will be important for you, not only for your clients but for yourself. Superb cooking, customer service, and problem-solving skills are more than necessary. Bring itemized meal plans with grocery lists to the store and try to familiarize yourself with the costs of common foods.

Realistic Expectations

Start with meal planning to learn the basics of how to put together a well-rounded meal. Teach yourself to not be wasteful with ingredients. Show up to meetings with meal plans to show off. Highlight the fact that you understand what nutritionally sound meals look like and know how to deal with allergens and cross-contamination in a kitchen. When you meet with clients you should cook something small for them to see your skill and talent for themselves. Make sure you understand all your client's likes and dislikes, and especially any food allergies, before you start building meal plans.

Making Bank

The average salary of a personal chef is $20.42 an hour.[77]

Business Equipment

The good news is that you'll be doing most of your cooking in other people's homes, so there isn't nearly as much startup cost as associated with

---

77. PayScale, 2017.

catering. You can use all of their utensils, but you would be wise to invest in a really good set of knives with a traveling case. A quality set of antimicrobial cutting boards that you know you'll use and clean in the proper way could be a good purchase. You'll also need reliable transportation so you can get to your clients and to the grocery store.

Marketing Tips

Word-of-mouth and customer testimonials on your marketing materials should do most of the work for you. Consider networking with local nutritionists and fitness centers to expand your visibility and client base.

Additional Resources

www.personalchef.com/personal_chef_faqs.php#.WJN6YVMrK00

www.whiteapronchef.com/steps-to-become-a-personal-chef/

www.cosmopolitan.com/career/a50984/things-i-wish-i-knew-before -i-became-a-personal-chef/

www.payscale.com/research/US/Job=Personal_Chef/Hourly_Rate

84. Cake Decorator

Business Overview

In the past couple of decades there have been reality shows that follow innovative cake decorators. If you've been inspired by these artists and you want to create gorgeous, whimsical, and creepy-looking cakes of your own, you can start now by becoming a self-employed cake decorator.

Education/Skills

There are no formal education requirements. You will need creativity, problem-solving, customer service, steady hands, and a sense of taste and smell. The ability to work within a budget and good food safety habits are also important. Get your hands on some how-to books and watch as many tutorials as you can to learn the basic tricks of the trade. Practice baking, piping, and fondant work until the techniques are second-nature, and your work is flawless.

Realistic Expectations

Take pictures of your best designs for your marketing materials. Food coloring, flour, and powdered sugar will make a mess of you most days, so get yourself an apron.

Making Bank

The average salary of a cake decorator is $11.76 an hour.[78]

Business Equipment

You'll need mixing bowls, measuring cups and spoons, spatulas, electric mixers, flavorings, colorings, and all kinds of other ingredients. You'll also need pans, an oven, a rolling pin, a candy thermometer, a large workspace, and sculpting tools of all kinds. Piping bags with every kind of tip, cardboard, dowels, and toothpicks are essential. Access to a dishwasher or large sink would be very helpful. You'll need a car with enough room to transport a big cake, and possibly some kind of rigging to make transportation smooth and uneventful. Bring a friend with steady hands on delivery days to help you move and assemble your masterpieces.

Marketing Tips

Use social media to share your best designs with the world. Imagine: your amazing cupcake design could be the next thing people fail at on Pinterest! Get testimonials from happy customers to use in your marketing materials. Partner with local venues and florists for big events, and with gourmet food shops for regular retail sales of smaller items like cupcakes.

Additional Resources

www.study.com/articles/Cake_Decorating_How_to_Be_a_Professional_Cake_Decorator.html

www.theartcareerproject.com/interview/rick-reichart/

---

78. PayScale, 2017.

www.payscale.com/research/US/Job=Cake_Decorator/Hourly_Rate

www.retailbakersofamerica.org/home.html

85.   Farmer's Market Food Seller

Business Overview

A farmer's market is a robust place with tons of options — if you've ever walked the aisles, you'll see everything from fresh fruit to baked bread to fully prepared meals. The signature of a farmer's market is that everything available is fresh and made with love.

Education/Skills

No education needed!

Realistic Expectations

You don't need any special advantages to join a farmer's market other than having something to sell.

Making Bank

How much you make depends on how much produce or products you have for sale. Are you competitively priced? How many people visit your local farmer's market? It's safe to expect a few hundred extra bucks in your pocket, but if you want to turn this into a full-fledged business, you'll have to continue your sales throughout the week by either opening a shop or by finding another way to sell your produce.

Business Equipment

To grow your produce, you'll need basic gardening equipment. To work in the farmer's market, you'll need at least a table and a cash drawer.

Marketing Tips

People need to start talking about your booth and how fresh and awesome your stuff is. Give out free samples to draw people in, and be very friendly.

Additional Resources

www.forbes.com/sites/moneybuilder/2012/04/11/how-to-make -money-at-the-farmers-market/#1e99c14526df

www.thekitchn.com/5-things-not-to-say-or-do-to-your-favorite -farmers-market-vendor-205359

www.mass.gov/eea/agencies/agr/markets/farmers-markets/farmers -market-howtorun-generic.html

86. Cooking Show Creator

Business Overview

To start your own cooking show, you'll need to create a YouTube channel. The idea is that you'll regularly post videos of your show, you're start to accumulate followers, and at some point you'll begin to make money through endorsements and maybe even by being picked up by a television network.

Education/Skills

You need to know how to cook. More importantly, you need to know how to cook and explain it to people. You need to make the videos interesting and entertaining. People may watch cooking shows to get recipe ideas or learn new techniques, but more often than not they're simply watching for entertainment. So, you need to be a good cook, a good teacher, and a good entertainer. You will have to have some camera skills. Close-ups, more than one shot, and careful editing are necessary to make the show interesting.

Realistic Expectations

There are many, many details to think about when starting a cooking show — and if you take them into consideration, you will be much more likely to be successful (video quality, food quality, entertainment quality, etc.). So if you're very good at cooking, explaining, and entertaining, you have a good shot of getting noticed.

Making Bank

The process of gathering followers and — eventually — making money will be slow. But if working on a cooking show in some capacity is what you want to do in the future, the experience will be invaluable.

CASE STUDY: CHASE BAILEY

Chase 'N Yur Face Media
Costa Mesa, CA
www.ChaseNYurFace.com

Chase 'N Yur Face Media officially started in 2013 when I was 12-years-old.

Long story short, I was diagnosed with autism when I was about 2 years old, and one of my symptoms was severe food aversions. When I was about 8 or 9, my grandfather and I found the cooking channels on TV. Watching the shows made me more comfortable with food because I could learn about food without having to smell, touch, or taste anything. After watching for a while, I decided to start trying new foods and making up recipes. From there I came up with the idea of maybe doing my own cooking show. Then finally, one day I thought, "I can do this!" One of my uncles said that he thought I should have a show called, "Chase in Your Face." From there, we came up with "Chase 'N Yur Face," and the rest is history!

I love seeing the ideas that I have in my head, come to life. I feel proud, creative, and independent. I also enjoy all the interesting people that I get to work with, experiencing new places, and eating delicious food.

I have an office in my home, and I can get most everything done with just a computer and a phone. Filming-days require a film crew that we hire for a few hours. We also hire other people from time to time to help with special projects. Right now, we only have one employee working for us. I'm lucky to have a big family and lots of people who care about me so I can get the help of volunteers when necessary.

Every time something that's been in my mind finally comes to life, those are all very satisfying moments. And when they happen, I'm usually already thinking about or working on the next ideas. But I have to say that two of the biggest highlights so far have been releasing my first cookbook — *The Official Chase 'N Yur Face Cookbook: Tasty Recipes & Fun Facts to Start Your Food Adventure* — and establishing the Chase Yur Dreams Foundation.

I have this process I call, "Check It Out, Get Up & Go, Make It Happen." What that means is you find something that you love and can't stop thinking about, you do as much research as you can about it; create a plan; and ask for help! None of us can do everything all by ourselves. We're all doing life with a little bit of help. It's important to surround yourself with people who support you and your ideas.

Business Equipment

You'll need a kitchen, of course, and all the necessary food and kitchen supplies.

Marketing Tips

You need to have a good name. The name needs to capture imaginations and make people want to watch you cook. You also need to think carefully about what you will wear. Have you ever noticed that cooking show hosts have really nice wardrobes? Maybe you could wear a signature apron — a look that could become part of your "brand."

Additional Resources

www.ifood.tv/reviews/300-the-stuff-about-making-a-cooking-show -that-nobody-tells-you

87.   Candy-maker

Business Overview

You could spread happiness by selling magically delicious candies that you make from scratch.

Education/Skills

Working with chocolate and candies requires a similar skill set to baking. There are different techniques to master, but ultimately the skills and abilities required are the same: creativity, problem-solving, customer service, steady hands, a sense of taste and smell, the ability to work within a budget, and good food safety habits. Watch tutorials, read how-to books, and practice your technique until you're comfortable and confident.

Realistic Expectations

If you take only custom orders, your income will be somewhat unpredictable. If you want something steadier you can make candies to sell in a retail establishment, at local gift shops or gourmet food stores. A combination of the two will provide you with the most income, but if you can't fit all that into your schedule right now, be honest with yourself and your customers about it. Holidays are going to be your blockbuster times of the year. Try to get as much prepped in advance as you can.

Making Bank

The average salary of a candy maker is $9.61 an hour.[79]

Business Equipment

You'll need a wide assortment of chocolate and different sugars in bulk sizes. Other necessities are flavorings, food coloring, molds, a candy thermometer and candy tools, corn starch, waxed paper, mixers, bowls, measuring cups and spoons, spatulas, pots and pans, cookie sheets and cooling racks, double-boilers, a stove, a sink, and a large ergonomic workspace.

---

79. Chron, 2014.

You'll need storage space for all your ingredients,and refrigeration to keep both ingredients and finished products in peak condition.

Marketing Tips

Use social media whenever possible, and get customer reviews and testimonials for your marketing materials. Approach local gourmet food stores and gift shops about selling your product on commission. Whenever you meet with a prospective client, bring a few samples of your most popular items, and photos of your best work.

Additional Resources

www.moneycrashers.com/how-to-start-candy-making-business/

www.smallbusiness.chron.com/start-home-based-candy-making -business-4328.html

www.99businessideas.com/home-based-candy-making-business/

www.work.chron.com/salary-candy-shop-owner-29353.html

www.insidejobs.com/careers/candy-maker

88.   Food Truck Owner/Operator

Business Overview

There's something about a food truck that appeals to the American spirit of independence: driving around, bringing delicious food to the masses. If you are creative and driven, and you've got some business acumen, you could make an excellent living as the owner of a food truck.

Education/Skills

On the administrative side of the business, running a food truck is like running a restaurant, only it's smaller and portable. Excellent food safety habits and knowledge is required. Your truck will be inspected by your state's Board of Health and given a grade. You will be required by your state to get special licenses and certifications to operate your truck: a business license and possibly a special type of driver's license; and food safety, health, and fire certifications. The culinary side requires cooking ability, problem-solving, meal planning, market awareness, and budgeting skills.

Realistic Expectations

Legally, you can't operate any part of the business out of your home, so you'll have to rent commercial kitchen space from a restaurant or commissary in your area. Food prep and cooking can be messy (hence the state inspections), and it will require physical stamina and strength. You can't just park your truck anywhere you want to and start slinging food out the window. You'll need to get permission from local businesses to park in their lots (a rental agreement may be necessary). It would be a good idea to check with your Chamber of Commerce and local business bureau about the rules and regulations regarding food truck operation in your area. You will also need business and auto insurance to cover yourself in the event of an accident. Check out **www.FoodTruckEmpire.com** for tips and resources.

Making Bank

The average salary of a food truck owner is $11.53 an hour.[80]

---

80. Indeed, 2017.

Business Equipment

Well, the first piece of equipment should be obvious: a truck! You'll need lots of food, storage for food, and all the tools and appliances you'd find in a commercial kitchen. You'll need a cash register and credit card processing equipment. You'll also need disposable (and hopefully recyclable) packaging and wrappers for the food you sell.

Marketing Tips

Make some menus and keep them updated, in print and online. Use social media to promote your menu and specials, as well as to let people in the area know where to find you.

Additional Resources

www.businessnewsdaily.com/9237-how-to-start-food-truck-business .html

www.foodtruckr.com/2013/10/what-i-wish-id-known-before-starting -my-food-truck/

www.priceonomics.com/post/45352687467/food-truck-economics

www.foodtruckempire.com/

Chapter 9

If You Have Muscles

89. Moving Services

Business Overview

The world is always on the move, no matter what. When the economy is booming, people move to better homes and better offices. When the economy isn't doing too hot, people move to smaller homes and smaller offices.

If you have the strength to move people's belongings, then you can start a moving business. And if you're not too keen on lifting heavy boxes and furniture, you can still use your sharp organizational skills to work as a moving assistant — the person who orchestrates the move and helps with packing and unpacking.

Education/Skills

While there are things like moving consultant certifications, there are no official requirements needed for this business.

Realistic Expectations

The moving industry is full of big and small competition. It will take a lot of time, hard work, and advertising to earn more than a supplemental income. If you have one or two strong employees and a moving vehicle, you might be surprised by how fast you get your first paying clients.

Making Bank

The average salary of a mover is $13.17 an hour.[81]

---

81. PayScale, 2017.

Business Equipment

Common equipment needed in the moving industry includes boxes, tape, labels, dollies, bubble wrap, protective blankets, furniture pads, measuring tape, ropes, ramps, tie-down systems, and a moving vehicle.

Marketing Tips

Tell everyone you know that you're building a business and are looking to gain experience by helping someone move. You can also hand out business cards, put up posters in community centers, libraries, laundromats, and other places where people will see them. To get even more attention, create a blog or website, take out classified newspaper ads, ask for referrals from friends and family members, and announce your service on social media.

Additional Resources

www.themovingblog.com

www.movinglaborprofessionals.com

www.moving.com

90. Appliance/Furniture Deliverer

Business Overview

If you don't want to help people move all their stuff — i.e., you don't want to help them move — but you enjoy work that is physically strenuous and giving a helping hand, this job could be perfect for you.

Education/Skills

You need muscles for this job — and you need to know how to use them. Not only do you need to be able to lift a heavy thing, but also you need to be able to do it without straining yourself. You need to be conscientious and notice when the right side of the dryer is about to hit the wall as you carry it up the basement steps.

Realistic Expectations

You'll have to investigate how to fulfill the legal requirements for starting a company, and it may take a while before you start attracting many customers. Still, if you have a good reputation and good rates, people *will* call you about those appliances they just don't know how to get rid of.

Making Bank

The average salary for someone who delivers appliances/furniture is $12.23 an hour.[82]

Business Equipment

To handle transportation to and from homes to whenever the appliances or furniture are going, you'll probably need a truck. And you might need to get some friends to join in on your business — some appliances are nearly impossible for one person to lift, no matter how strong he or she is.

---

82. PayScale, 2017.

Marketing Tips

Sometimes, furniture delivery services don't operate on the weekends. This is a great opportunity for you. You could have more flexible and convenient hours than many other more-established moving companies do not.

Additional Resources

www.entrepreneur.com/businessideas/furniture-delivery-and -assembly

91. Organizer

Business Overview

As a professional organizer, you will be the life preserver that tugs those wayward souls back into the current, and teaches them how to avoid similar hazards in the future.

Education/Skills

Organization skills are an absolute must! You will also need to be productive, neat, and have a good sense of spatial awareness. Problem-solving, budgeting, and customer service skills will always serve you well. You don't need any certifications or training, though there are classes, websites, and books that will help you learn the tools of the trade.

Realistic Expectations

Your natural tendency toward order should be immediately evident to potential clients. If you have a meeting: show up on time, dress like a professional, come prepared to take notes, and bring before-and-after photos of previous work. You should always be aware that you are sorting through the physical representation of another person's life. Don't mistreat any item you handle.

Making Bank

The average salary of a professional organizer is $25.71 an hour.[83]

Business Equipment

Colored stickers, post-its, pens, paper, notebooks, a clipboard, storage bins, and a label maker are the basic supplies that will help you with any job. You will also need a vehicle to get to customers' homes and to the thrift store.

Marketing Tips

Your standard marketing materials will need to have a clean design and be uncluttered. Obtaining customer testimonials and before-and-after photos should be standard procedure.

Additional Resources

www.smallbusiness.chron.com/start-home-organizing-business-4257 .html

www.organize365.com/how-to-become-a-professional-organizer/

www.timetoorganize.com/about/career-faqs/

www.profitableorganizer.com/

www.angieslist.com/articles/what-do-professional-organizers-charge .htm

---

83. PayScale, 2017.

92. Junk Remover

Business Overview

All households slowly acquire junk that, at some point, has to be removed: computers, furniture, old sports equipment, refrigerators, washers and dryers, mattresses, and even tree stumps. If you have access to a van or truck, you can turn people's junk into an opportunity to make money.

Education/Skills

There are no educational requirements for this business. All you need is organizational skills, a driver's license, and the strength to lift heavy objects. However, the field can be tricky, so it would also be beneficial to familiarize yourself with local waste handling rules, regulations, and permits, as well as local dump sites and their associated costs.

Realistic Expectations

Although this is an easy business to start, the industry doesn't always provide a steady stream of work. You may go through periods of either feast or famine. Still, there are plenty of ways to optimize your profitable opportunities, such as offering your clients additional services, keeping an eye out for items that can be refurbished and resold, or hauling junk strictly as a side business while working at another job.

Making Bank

There are a lot of variables to consider when it comes to junk removal fees, including the distance to your client and what kind of material they need removed. Consider factors like fuel, time, and employees; be sure to research local and national junk removal companies to set a fair, but competitive rate.

Drive to your client and offer a free estimate — chances are you'll not only get the job, but you'll get a price you're more comfortable with.

Business Equipment

Common equipment needed in this industry includes a tough and spacious vehicle, dollies, measuring tape, ropes, ramps, tie-down systems, tarps, trailers, and red flags to put on the end of loads that extend beyond the end of the vehicle.

Marketing Tips

One type of client you should target? Local realtors that deal with foreclosures. These types of properties often have a lot of trash, debris, and other objects that need to be removed before the house is thrown back on the market; If you offer a fair price and do your job well, you may be recommended for similar jobs.

You can also hand out business cards, put up posters in community centers, libraries, and other places where people will see them. To get even more attention, take out classified newspaper ads, ask for referrals from friends and family members, announce your services on social media.

Additional Resources

www.haulawaycash.com

www.thebalance.com/starting-a-junk-removal-business-eight-things -to-consider-2877794

www.mysmallbiz.com/business-idea/junk-removal-business

93.   Automotive Detailer

Business Overview

Auto detailing can range anywhere from your standard wash and wax to applying custom art and tinted windows. It's a great business to start for artists and auto enthusiasts alike.

Education/Skills

To make the most out of this business, you should have some type of auto detailing background or education. If not, study some how-to books or videos, take a course supplied by adult education programs or local colleges, or try to get some experience by working for a local auto detailer before setting out on your own.

You should also check out *Fast Cash: The Young Adult's Guide to Detailing Cars, Boats, & RVs* by Atlantic Publishing Group, Inc. This book teaches the most efficient ways to start and run a full-time car detailing business with a minimal amount of money and in a minimal amount of time.

Realistic Expectations

One of the cool things about working with cars is the accessibility of the trade. You can run an express detailing business that just deals with the basics, run your business from home, join a franchise, take over an established detailing shop, look for work at an auto dealer, or hit the road as a mobile detail service.

Making Bank

The average salary of an automotive detailer is $10.94 an hour.[84]

Business Equipment

The type of equipment you need depends on the type of detailing services you offer. Some common tools include a pressure washer, a high-speed buffer, random orbital polisher, GEM orbital polisher, an air compressor, a carpet extractor, wet/dry vacuum, ozone odor remover, odor fogger system, and an interior dryer.

Marketing Tips

Visit different shops and neighborhoods to hand out fliers that describe your business as well as your special promotions. This will allow you to introduce yourself to potential customers, get the word out, and show off your skills.

You can also stand on the side of the road with a sign directing cars to your site or put up posters in community centers, libraries, and other places where people will see them. To get even more attention, take out classified newspaper ads, ask for referrals from friends and family members, announce your services on social media.

Additional Resources

www.autogeek.net

www.autopia.org

www.chemicalguys.com

---

84. PayScale, 2017.

94. Snow Shoveler

Business Overview

As a snow shoveler, you will remove snow from driveways and sidewalks as well as dig out cars from the snow. Some snow shovelers also offer salt laying as an additional service.

Education/Skills

There are no educational requirements for this business, but you should have the strength, stamina, and know-how needed for shoveling snow.

Realistic Expectations

If you love working outside and are only looking for a supplementary income, then snow shoveling is perfect for you.

Making Bank

How much you charge for shoveling snow will depend on your location, the size of the job, and your competition. For a standard two-car driveway, snow shovelers can expect to make anywhere between $10 and $50 dollars an hour, with an additional charge added if you are laying salt as well.

Business Equipment

For a standard snow shoveling business, you can get by with warm clothes and a snow shovel. But if you are taking on a lot of jobs and want to get a leg up on the competition, you might also want to invest in a snow blower and animal- and eco-friendly rock salt.

Marketing Tips

Visit different shops and neighborhoods to hand out fliers that describe your business as well as any special promotions you may have.

You can also put up posters in community centers, libraries, and other places where people will see them. To get even more attention, take out classified newspaper ads, ask for referrals from friends and family members, and announce your services on social media.

Additional Resources

www.snowmagazineonline.com

www.moneypantry.com/make-money-shoveling-snow

www.geos-school.com/how-to-start-a-snow-removal-business

95.   Lawn Service

Business Overview

With a lawn care business, you will be responsible for all sorts of lawn maintenance. These duties often include cutting grass, pulling weeds, trimming trees and bushes, raking pine straw and leaves, blowing excess grass from sidewalks and driveways, and doing other landscaping tasks.

Education/Skills

There are no educational requirements, but you will need a basic knowledge of plant care and pest control, as well as the ability to install sod and operate lawn care equipment like mowers, leaf blowers, hedge trimmers, and chainsaws.

Realistic Expectations

According to the 2015 Bureau of Labor Statistics, there are over 1.28 million people employed as grounds maintenance workers in the United States alone; this number is projected to increase by six percent in 2024.

Making Bank

The average salary of a landscaper is $12.05 an hour.[85]

Business Equipment

Some common equipment needed for lawn care includes commercial lawnmowers, blowers, hedge cutters, edgers, weed whacker, rakes, fuel for your equipment, and a truck or trailer to haul everything.

---

85. PayScale, 2017.

Marketing Tips

You can hand out business cards, put up posters in neighborhoods, community centers, libraries, and other places where people will see them. To get even more attention, take out classified newspaper ads, ask for referrals from friends and family members, and announce your services on social media.

Additional Resources

www.fixr.com/costs/lawn-maintenance

www.thebalance.com/pros-and-cons-of-starting-a-lawn-business -1794497

www.lawndoctor.com

96.   Gardening Service

Business Overview

If you love gardening and helping people out, this could be the perfect job for you. Basically, you will go over to someone else's house and work in his or her garden — probably for a few hours a day.

Education/Skills

Some basic horticultural knowledge is required. You'll probably have to have some physical strength and endurance to garden for several hours each day, because it is strenuous work!

Realistic Expectations

This may not be a full-time, eight-hours-a-day job, but at the same time, it could be a steady job for after school and the summers for many years.

Making Bank

The average salary of a gardener is $15.33 an hour.[86]

Business Equipment

Your client will probably have all the tools you need, but some gardening gloves that fit your hands well would be a good investment.

Marketing Tips

You are most likely to get this job from word-of-mouth inquiries. So if you're interested in a job like this, don't be scared to ask your neighbor if he or she would like an extra pair of hands to work in the garden.

86. PayScale, 2017.

Chapter 10

In Case You *Still* Haven't Found Your Niche

97. Astrologer

Business Overview

If you enjoy the mystery of the celestial bodies and how they can relate to different people, being an astrologer is the perfect job for you.

Education/Skills

Although no education is required for this job, you will need to be familiar with zodiac signs and astrology charts and how to read them, as well as other psychic techniques like cold reading.

Realistic Expectations

Over 40 percent of Americans believe that astrology is at least a little scientific — 120 million potential clients in the U.S. alone. Whether it's for fun or for serious business decisions, every city has people who are interested in getting a professional astrology reading, and the internet has even more.

Making Bank

The average salary of an astrologer is $32.86 an hour.[87]

Business Equipment

At the very least, you will need astrological books and charts and a specific space dedicated to your business. Some astrologers may also need a digital recorder, computer, printer, telephone, and astrological software.

Marketing Tips

Give your astrology business a professional, mystical name and create a flyer that accurately describes your rates and services. Visit different shops and neighborhoods to hand them out.

You can also put up posters in community centers, libraries, and other places where people will see them. To get even more attention, ask for referrals from friends and family members, announce your services on social media.

If you understand the core concept of putting an astrological chart together, you can also start by contacting newspapers, magazines, or local publications to offer your services in their paper on a monthly, weekly, or daily basis.

Additional Resources

www.opaastrology.org

www.skyscript.co.uk

www.astrosoftware.com/AstroBusiness.htm

---

87. SimplyHired, 2017.

98.   Talent Agent

Business Overview

A talent agent is someone who represents any type of talent. Most specifically, talent agents typically represent a band, artist, or an actor.

Education/Skills

You don't necessarily have to have a degree, but a degree might help add a lot of insight into the field. If you don't get a degree, it might be helpful to take marketing classes so you can learn how best to get the band of whom you are representing out there. The more business your client gets, the more you can make.

Realistic Expectations

If you know of someone who has a band, it would be an easy start to represent them and help them book gigs. Some agents work their way to representing multiple people, but it would be best to start with one client and see where that leads.

Making Bank

The average salary of a talent agent is $12 an hour.[88]

Business Equipment

You don't require any equipment in particular, but it might be helpful to have a smartphone and a computer to make calls and send emails.

---

88. PayScale, 2017

Marketing Tips

Contact local bands to see if they are looking for an agent. Make a website so people can send inquiries.

Additional Resources

www.unitedtalent.com/

99.   Mystery/Secret Shopping Specialist

Business Overview

Companies and restaurants hire mystery shoppers to rate the employee/shopper relationship, the store's cleanliness, and a variety of other issues the store has had complaints or concerns about.

Education/Skills

There is no educational degree needed. Good communication skills and customer relations experience are helpful.

Realistic Expectations

You'll probably be able to get some jobs if you seem credible. The difficulty might be in getting steady, consistent work.

Making Bank

You'll probably make $5 to $25 per trip. That's a small sum, of course, but if you're able to pick up jobs, that could be a tidy weekly sum.

Business Equipment

You might want to purchase a database software program to keep track of each shop you have rated, along with the ratings and comments for future use. You will also want to keep track of the businesses that have used your service in the past.

Marketing Tips

Contact businesses nationally who have chain stores in your area and announce your business. Let them know your prices and your methods for shopping or dining out (how you plan to rate the services and such). You can also put together a website and advertise online with various business and office product stores.

Additional Resources

www.teensgotcents.com/mystery-shopper-jobs-teens/

100. Consignment Shop Owner

Business Overview

Running a consignment shop means you will need to rent a storefront, or you can run an online consignment shop via Etsy, Instagram, etc. Many consignment shop owners purchase clothes that are free of stains and rips for a small fee from clients, and then they increase the price when they put it on the racks to sell.

Education/Skills

You should understand the day-to-day operations of running a business, but other than that knowledge you need no additional degrees or skills.

Realistic Expectations

The main problem here will be getting the supplies and in distinguishing your consignment shop from all the others that are undoubtedly sprinkled throughout your city.

Making Bank

The average salary of a consignment shop owner is $13.32 an hour.[89]

---

89. PayScale, 2017.

CASE STUDY: BAKER DONAHUE

In With the Old began in the Summer of 2016—the result of two broke, bored college students looking for something exciting to take on.

The idea came from a lack of stylish clothing around the University of Tennessee campus. The people who stood out on game day were those who were wearing the flashy one-of-a-kind vintage apparel. I realized there was no centralized market to purchase these items aside from thrift stores or sketchy online transactions. After realizing we couldn't afford to pay for a website, we took our idea to Instagram. We put an emphasis on aesthetically pleasing images and funky branding. The picture was the product, the caption was the description of the product, and the comments are the bids.

In With the Old is a very profitable business. Our average product cost is around $10, and we usually see an 80 percent increase on selling price.

In the wise words of Nike, "Just Do It." The hardest part about starting your own business is deciding you want to start you own business. The risk is pretty high — you're using your own money and your own ideas, all of which are susceptible to judgment and critique. When I told my friends I wanted to sell vintage clothing off of Instagram, they all thought it was a good idea, but never envisioned me actually doing something with it. All of us have some idea stewing around that could potentially change the course of our lives. Take the initial leap of faith, and just give it a shot. What's the worst thing that could happen?

Baker Donahue is a junior at the University of Tennessee, majoring in communication studies with a minor in entrepreneurship.

Business Equipment

Clothing racks, cash register, counter space, a steam cleaner, and other display equipment will be needed. Even if you're running this at home, you'll obviously need some storage space for the clothing.

Marketing Tips

Rent a small flea market space and begin selling the clothes you received from the clothing drive. Or start an Instagram account for your store for a few weeks, see what works and doesn't work, and learn from it.

Additional Resources:

www.smallbusiness.chron.com/start-online-consignment-store-4699 .html

101.   Product Manufacturer

Business Overview

Is your dream job to make something—to create a totally new type of product? It could be a new tool to help slice avocados—or it could be a coat made of a new combination of synthetic material. The options are endless.

Education/Skills

You don't need a degree, but you need a strong work ethic and perseverance. Designing a new product on your own as a teen is a big feat. You need both a creative mind that can focus on developing something new as well as a practical side that will help you bring it to execution.

Realistic Expectations

Most new patents don't make any money. Realize that even if you go to all the work to create your new product, the odds are that it might not make a cent.

Making Bank

The average salary of a product manufacturer is $18.51 an hour.[90]

CASE STUDY: MATT SHUMER (CO-CEO) AND RYAN COHN (CHIEF CHARITY OFFICER)

FURI
New York, NY
www.furisport.com

We started creating FURI in November 2015, when we both were 15.

A year and a half ago, Matt was planning to start a tennis e-commerce website. As he was making deals with some of the big tennis manufacturers to sell their products, they were sending him their pricing sheets. Soon, he started noticing a trend between all of the brands. They all sold products that were extremely cheap to make (around $25-$50) for very high prices (as much as $300+). Matt knew he had to do something about it, so he pivoted and shifted his efforts to start a manufacturing company instead. Soon after, he realized he couldn't do this alone, so he contacted Ryan (his best friend) and asked him to join. In the time since, the team has grown to over 7 people, most being business professionals from NYC.

We will begin to sell our accessories in November on our e-commerce store, and at different events, as well as selling our tennis rackets starting in 2017. Also, based on the start-up costs and manufacturing, we do not project to be profitable until the end of year 3.

---

90. PayScale, 2017.

We are both currently in 11th grade, which is informally known by teenagers as "Hell Year" due to the huge amounts of tests, projects, and general workload that is given to us this year, accompanied by tests like the ACT and SAT. It is incredibly tough to juggle all of this on its own, never mind starting FURI. We work a LOT. We spend the hours between 7:00 am and 2:15 pm at school. When we get home, we do our homework and study (depending on the day this could be anywhere from 1 hour to 5 hours of more work). After this, we start working on whatever needs to get done for FURI. This is really tough, but worth it.

Matt: My most satisfying moment as a teen entrepreneur would definitely have to be the day that we tried out our first prototype rackets. That was the day that I realized that we really had something in FURI, not just a bunch of social media followers and a website.

Ryan: My most satisfying moment as a teen entrepreneur was the moment when we placed our first product order. This was super satisfying because it meant that we now had something to offer to the world. It transformed FURI from "just an idea" to something more — something tangible.

We know that it may be a lot of work (it is!), but if you have an idea and enough drive, you can do it. Also, don't do it if it's just for the money. If you're just being driven by money, you will lose interest quickly, and the business will fail. One of our main goals is to provide access to sports to anyone that wants to play, and that goal has kept us on track and motivated us to keep going day after day. Also, don't listen to anyone that says that you can't do it. Prove them wrong. If we listened to the dozens of people that told us that we would fail if we tried this, we would not be doing this today.

Business Equipment

Your business equipment needs will vary greatly.

Marketing Tips

Get your idea thoroughly evaluated by friends, family members, and any relevant experts that you may be able to connect with. Research whether or not there is demand for it.

Additional Resources

www.smallbusiness.chron.com/make-own-products-sell-distribute -67434.html

Chapter 11

How to Finance Your Business

One of the major questions you and other entrepreneurs like you are asking is, "What do investors look for?" The answer to that question is simple: a good idea and an individual who can exploit that idea well.

An investor's decision relies heavily on the execution of your business plan; if your business plan is not written well, an investor will close the door on your idea. Even if you have a well thought out plan and have prepared it satisfactorily, the number of plans that make it to final approval are very low. For the thousands of business plans that are placed on investors' desks only about 500 business plans are examined carefully. Of those 500 plans only around 25 are pursued to the negotiation stage and from there only about six or so are actually invested in.[91]

Investors want to know that your product or service is in demand or is currently being used. You should test your business out without putting any money out or before you dig into starting your business. Doing so will show potential investors how your product was used, considered, and how much the clients enjoyed it. Be sure to get a short questionnaire to the clients and get pictures, or evidence, of your product or service's effect on the

91. C. Barrow, P. Barrow, and Brown, 2012.

client or business. Apply all this information to your business plan to help potential investors make a more positive decision about investing in you and your product.

When you do contact investors make sure the following questions can be answered:

 What type of money do you need?

 How much money to you need? What will that money be used for specifically? Such as:

- $2,000 for a computer system

- $10,000 for employee startup

- $600 for a digital camera

- Make each money need as detailed as possible to give the investor a complete picture of your needs.

 When will you need the money?

 What are you offering your investors in return?

 When will the money be paid back to your investors? What type of return will be given?

 What exit routes are offered to the investors?

Forms of Financing

There are a few forms of financing that can help your company get off the ground faster and give you a better chance of succeeding.

Borrow startup funds from friends and family

Asking for money from friends and family can be tricky, but they will be some of your biggest supporters and believe in you more than a random stranger on the street will. It can be tricky, with no credit built up, to receive a loan from a bank, but you may know some people around you who want to invest in you, your business, and your future.

Consider crowdfunding

Crowdfunding has become more and more popular over the years. Post your business idea on a site like **www.GoFundMe.com** and you may be surprised with how many people like your idea and want to donate money to help you start your business. Sites like GoFundMe can also just make collecting money and spreading the word about your idea a little easier.

Look into peer-to-peer lending

This can be another great way to receive a loan without going through the bank. A person looking to start a business, you, fills out an online application. Once the application is completed a lender looks over your application and provided you with a loan offer along with an interest rate. For more information on this process, go to **https://www.fundingcircle.com/ us/resources/basics-of-peer-to-peer-lending/**

Additional Forms of Financing

Just because you would rather not go through a bank or investment company, do not throw aside these other thoughts on financing without considering them thoroughly.

Personal Savings

Having personal savings can help you get on track. When starting a business there is no better time to take that out and use it. Sometimes you have to spend money to make money.

Other Business Owners

Other business owners in your area could also be a good place to seek out small loan amounts. They were once in your shoes attempting to gain the necessary money to make their dreams come true. If you will be getting a loan from other business owners, you will have to legalize everything and have a lawyer draw papers up indicating the loan amount, interest amount, and repayment details.

Grants for Small Businesses

There are grants available for your small business, but be aware of the scams associated with them. Grant information is available for you free of charge at any local library. You will have to go to the library's grantsmanship center, which is normally located in the business and resources section. Ask a librarian for help.

To research grants online you can check out the following websites:

www.gpoaccess.gov/fr/index.html

www.foundationcenter.org/pnd/21century

www.12.46.245.173/cfda/cfda.html

http://usgovinfo.about.com/library/weekly/blgrantsources.htm

www.grantsmart.org

www.internet-prospector.org

Business Tips, Information, and Resources for Students

Q&A: Small Business and the SEC

A guide to help you understand how to raise capital and comply with the federal securities laws: **www.sba.com**.

SCORE - Service Corps of Retired Executives

The Service Corps of Retired Executives (SCORE) provides information about the organization and its services, a directory of SCORE chapters across the United States, online workshops, and e-mail counseling services, feature articles, and success stories: **http://www.score.org/**.

Inc. offers daily resources for entrepreneurs: **http://www.inc.com**.

Entrepreneur Mag offers a ton of resources and links for those starting or expanding a business: **www.entrepreneurmag.com**.

Association of Collegiate Entrepreneurs: **http://oak.cats.ohiou.edu/~ace /index.html**.

A nonprofit organization dedicated to supporting students preparing for careers in business and business-related fields: **http://www.fbla-pbl.org**

Offers resources to the business needs of Generation X entrepreneurs with information, advice, and fun: **http://www.businessownersideacafe.com /genx**.

Profiles of business owners who started their businesses as students, along with numerous resources for young entrepreneurs: **http://www.inc .com/search/20808.html**.

Provided to educate and inspire young people to value free enterprise, business, and economics to improve the quality of their lives: **http://www .ja.org**.

Kauffman Entrepreneur Internship Program: **http://www.keip.org**.

Kidpreneurs: **http://www.blackenterprise.com/PageOpen.asp?Source =KidpreneursLink/kidkonference.htm**

Offers middle and high school students with advice, quizzes, pro and con discussions of business ownership, and other business education resources: **http://www.usmint.gov/kids/**.

The organization offers micro-enterprise development assistance, conferences, youth entrepreneur awards, technical assistance, and more: **http://www.agnr.umd.edu/users/kidbiz/nceyehist.html**

NFTEs: **http://www.nfte.com**

Students in Free Enterprise (SIFE): **http://www.sife.org**

YoungBiz: **http://www.youngbiz.com.**

Young Entrepreneur: **http://www.youngentrepreneur.com/.**

Young Entrepreneurs Network: **http://www.youngandsuccessful.com.**

Young Entrepreneurs' Organization (YEO): **http://www.yeo.org/.**

Resources for young entrepreneurs, who want to start, run, or grow their businesses: **http://www.sba.gov/teens.**

Youth Venture: **http://www.youthventure.org.**

Financing - Where to Apply for and Get Your Financing

America's Business Funding Directory

This commercial site provides a searchable database of potential lenders or investors for businesses, along with other information and resources related to funding: **http://www.businessfinance.com.**

SBA: Financing Your Business

The U.S. Small Business Administration works with banks and other institutions to provide loans and venture capital financing to businesses unable to secure financing through normal lending channels; this page describes the various programs available: **http://www.sbaonline.sba.gov/financing/**.

Conclusion

This book is packed full of business ideas from cooking to editing and everything in between! We hope that you found one that suits you! Maybe you even learned about a business that you didn't even know existed.

Hopefully after reading through this book, you feel confident enough to start a business of your own and are equipped with all the tools you need to get your business up and running! We know that starting a business can be a scary venture, but you never know how successful you can be until you got out into the world and try! Be sure to go back and read some of the case studies from people just like you who had an idea, went for it, and found themselves owners of great and profitable businesses. Don't let anyone tell you that you are too young to start a business because we found people who show that just simply isn't true.

One of the best things about owning a business? There is truly nothing like being your own boss.

Make sure you know exactly what you want your business to be before you start crafting your business plan and looking for loans. You want to be sure that you are confident in your idea and know exactly what you want so that an investor won't influence you or make you change your business idea more than you are comfortable with.

This book is packed with information, so feel free to continue to reference this book as you continue to build your businesses. Make sure to also check out some of the additional resources listed under the various business ideas listed in this book. Before you know it, you will have a booming business!

Bibliography

"Analyzing Babysitter Price & Gender Data." *Priceonomics*, 14 Mar. 2014.

"Astrology Salaries." *Simply Hired*, 2017.

Barrow, Colin, Paul Barrow, and Robert Brown. *The Business Plan Workbook*. 7th ed., Philadelphia, Kogan Page, 2012.

"Candle Maker Salary in United States." *Salary Expert*, Economic Research Institute, Inc., 2017.

Chron, Hearst Newspapers, LLC, 2017.

"Food Truck Manager Salaries in the United States." *Indeed*, 15 July 2017.

GlassDoor, 2017.

"House Cleaning Services - Average Prices & Costs." *HomeAdvisor*, 2015.

PayScale, 2017.

Pinola, Melanie. "Can I Really Make a Living by Blogging?." *Life Hacker*, 6 Mar. 2014.

"Salary and Career Info for a Greeting Card Designer." *Study*, 2017.

Smith, Tiffany. "How Much Should You Pay Your Sitter?." *Care*, 2017.

U.S. Bureau of Labor Statistics, 2017.

Williams, RN, DC, Dr. Mary. "How Much Does a CPR Class Cost & Is it Worth the Investment?." *CPR Certified*, 14 Aug. 2015.

Index

A

Advertise 24, 30, 36, 38, 109, 114, 146, 160, 163, 176, 186, 237

B

Business cards   24, 30, 41, 46, 63, 69, 76, 91, 95, 102, 104, 108, 149, 157, 160, 177, 179, 183, 187, 219, 224, 230

C

Campaigns 48, 155, 195

Certification 39, 42, 56, 94, 142, 147, 165

Communication 33, 68, 71, 78, 87, 92, 96, 101, 119, 130, 156, 159, 162, 237, 239

Competition 21, 23, 26, 51, 123, 173, 174, 181, 186, 188, 194, 218, 227

Costs 6, 23, 51, 75, 131, 135, 137, 159, 165, 204, 223, 230, 241, 255

Creativity 45, 75, 92, 94, 96, 98, 113, 181, 198, 206, 213

Crowdfunding 135, 140, 247

D

Demand 20, 25, 31, 94, 143, 243, 245

Discount 52, 100

E

Events 76, 92, 95, 97, 101, 111, 132, 143, 146, 150, 151, 180, 182, 203, 207, 241

Expense 159

F

Field 33, 65, 67, 70, 73, 74, 78, 92, 158, 184, 223, 235

Finance 10, 127, 245

I

Income 13, 16, 20, 31, 40, 67, 70,
    98, 117, 159, 213, 218, 227
Industry 51, 68, 69, 72, 85, 86,
    90, 110, 132, 135, 160, 170,
    181, 183, 218, 219, 223, 224
Insurance 24, 39, 49, 215
Investment 12, 19, 26, 105, 231,
    247, 256
Investors 245, 246, 251

L

Licensing 4, 186
Loan 15, 247, 248

N

Networking 29, 46, 111, 205

O

Organizations 5, 22, 142, 143, 164
Overhead 37, 49, 176, 178, 186

P

Portfolio 64, 67, 104, 105, 116,
    131, 160, 162, 183
Pricing 41, 49, 241
Process 15, 46, 58, 59, 79, 122,
    162, 199, 210-212, 247

Profitable 34, 35, 70, 75, 133, 148,
    164, 176, 193, 223, 239, 241,
    253

Q

Questionnaire 19, 21, 245

R

Referrals 27, 30, 32, 36, 44, 53,
    70, 76, 109, 149, 157, 177, 179,
    183, 187, 219, 224, 226, 228,
    230, 234
Relationships 37, 50, 126
Résumé 19, 31, 70

S

Sample 56
Schedule 4-16, 19, 41, 60, 85, 92,
    213
Self-employment 5, 13, 16
Startup 15, 23, 51, 105, 129, 204,
    246, 247
Syndicate 88

T

Tax
9, 16, 22, 37, 185-187
Transportation 41, 75, 141, 143,
    144, 164, 165, 202, 205, 207,
    220

W

Word-of-mouth 46, 74, 116, 120, 170, 202, 205, 231